GlobeWandering on a Budget

Travel Tips for Grown-ups

Copyright © 2018 by Kinnisonic, Inc. All rights reserved. This book or any portion thereof may not be reproduced or used in any manner whatsoever without the express written permission of the publisher except for the use of brief quotations in a book review.

What People Are Saying

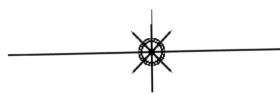

"I travel for a living and still found lots of useful and unique travel advice in this book. Carrie's comfortable style and her engaging anecdotes make for an entertaining read. Her encouragement to make connections with locals is spot on. Cheers!"

~ Jack Maxwell

Dedication

To my Mom and Dad, who taught me the joys of traveling in foreign lands from the time I was a baby. I'm a traveler because of you.

To the wonderfully kind, interesting, and crazy people I've met while traveling. I wrote this book so that others can have similar remarkable experiences with people like you.

And to Pat, my ever-patient soulmate, love of my life, and GlobeWandering companion. I wouldn't be complete without you.

Foreword

By: Pat Kinnison

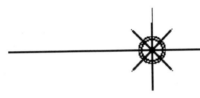

When Every Day Becomes a Magic Carpet Ride

Travel is magical. It arouses the senses in the same way that a great work of fiction immerses you in another place and time, compelling you to turn the page to see what's next, enticing you to read just one more page before bed.

Like reading, travel is a learned skill with multiple facets. *How* to travel and *why* you should travel are two distinctly different things that must be learned and developed. *How* is simply the means to the end, involving such skills as finding lodging or transportation. It is something that is required in order to experience the magic. *How* also requires expenditure, and unless you have unlimited funds to explore properly and comfortably, you'll need to work within the framework of a fixed budget, which requires an extensive amount of practical know-how, knowledge attained through years of boots-on-the-ground travel. Carrie has that knowledge.

A methodical electrical engineer (she will read "geek" into that statement), Carrie expertly and uniquely puts on paper how to prepare before exploring magical lands and cultures. To Carrie, the *how* is not drudgery; rather, it is an opportunity to learn, to enjoy the accomplishment of mastering a new skill. In other words, it's fun. And that comes through in her presentation. To revel in the magic of travel, you must first live modestly and save, save, save. Then, when an opportunity presents itself, or you simply get the urge, you'll have the financial means to fulfill your dream, and you won't need to wait until retirement.

Although essential before embarking on an adventure, the *how* is only a part of the required skill set. Equally, the *why* is critical in deciding not only where you should go, but also how much time you will need in order to meet your goals, and what type of cultural interaction you want and expect. And that is where Carrie truly shines. With an obvious joie de vivre, she provides the reader with real-life insights based on experiences which I was lucky enough to share with her. In this guide, she carefully delineates what can be achieved with proper planning, a can-do attitude, and a willingness to venture beyond your comfort zone. Carrie's advice and anecdotes will provide inspiration for *why* you ought to travel, but in no way does she absolve you from doing your own soul-searching. *Why* you want to wander is still a deeply personal matter, and the impetus to do so is different for everyone.

To say that her level of experience in all forms of travel is extensive is an understatement, and I can attest to that having been party to most of it. It all began shortly after I proposed to her in 1991. I recall that we were at our favorite sushi bar — actually the only sushi bar — in Flagstaff, Arizona, when I asked Carrie, "Hey, where do you want to go on our honeymoon?" "Do you remember the adventure travel brochure from Mountain Travel that I showed you?" she said. I nodded. "Let's go to Nepal and trek the Himalayas," she continued. I smiled. "OK!" And that set the hook. We started saving money for the next trip, then for the trip after that, then, well you get the idea.

Our next travel/life milestone was a trip to Tonga. A friend and his wife, knowing that we sailed a little 14-foot sailboat on Flagstaff's mountain lakes, invited us to join them and two other couples on a bareboat sailing trip to Tonga. Without hesitation, we answered with an enthusiastic yes.

Call us crazy, but shortly after that trip we sold everything, bought a blue-water cruising sailboat, and moved aboard her in San Diego, California. For five years in San Diego we honed our sailing skills, which were at first nearly nonexistent, and then for the following five years we cruised Mexico, Central America, and South America. Memories? Yes, as you might expect, we have many. The places we saw, many of which are rarely frequented by tourists, were awe-inspiring, but that was only the sidebar. It was the people met, the bonds created through shared experiences, that really made our nomadic lifestyle special. That is *why* we travel.

A great deal of the travel that we did during our sailing years was actually inland. We would find a safe place to moor the boat, then Carrie would work her transportation and lodging magic, and I would make sure we had a way of accessing funds when needed and that we stayed within budget. These little trips lasted between one and three months. At first, our travel was clunky, sometimes uncomfortable, even a bit frustrating, but we always made it fun and learned from each event. Carrie believes that it's all about attitude, and she writes extensively about how important a proper attitude is to successful free-form travel. As time went on — and as we became older — our travel became smoother, more comfortable, much less frustrating. Our blog posts back then were also a bit rough. We hope, too, that our writing skills have improved as much as our travel skills. Visit our blog, vinohiking.com, to experience our evolutionary process, and let us know what you think.

A recurring theme throughout the book is that the relationships we developed, the new friendships that we acquired, were as rewarding or even more rewarding than scratching an iconic site off our bucket list, but as the book is based on pairs traveling, how traveling can affect your relationship with your companion is also an important consideration. Obviously, the key here is that a strong bond must exist from the beginning. With that said, it can still go either way. After all, the nomadic lifestyle requires that the couple live, work and play, usually in tight quarters, with little space to get away. The standard joke between Carrie and me is that "we're never more than five feet apart." A constant within this lifestyle is that you're continually bombarded with new challenges, always learning new skills, invariably immersed in new cultures and languages, and forever in unique and unfamiliar places. During those times, you learn a great deal about your partner, as well as about yourself. And one such event occurred very early on in the sailing portion of our alt-lifestyle.

We left Ensenada, Mexico, December 28th, 2005, under a weather forecast that promised 15 to 20 knots of wind from the northwest. Perfect conditions as we were heading southeast to Cabo San Lucas. Shortly after sundown, the wind picked up to a consistent 25 knots and the seas became uncomfortable. A few hours later, the wind was a consistent 40+ knots and the roar of the waves was deafening. We reefed (shortened sail), yet we were still going too fast, making the boat a little uncontrollable and squirrely. Sleep was impossible. I sat at the helm, keeping a vigilant eye on the auto-pilot. If it was overpowered, the boat could turn sideways to a wave and be pushed over. We nearly went over once and were pooped another time (overtaken by a large breaking wave — water filling the cockpit). This lasted for 48 hours, with both of us hallucinating towards the end due to sleep deprivation. As the sun set on the second night, I was reminded of our Nepal trip, with the white-tipped waves reminiscent of the Himalayas. There was no opportunity for panic. We both knew what was required, and we went about those tasks with a determined and focused purpose. If that's not a bond-building event, then I don't know what is. And from there, with each new challenge our bond increased. Perhaps that's the definition of soulmate — a person with whom you form an unbreakable bond that continues to grow with each new experience. And ultimately, that's the gift received by accepting this lifestyle. Now, our combatting the gale was an extreme case, but rest assured, you will learn new things about your partner during your free-form traveling and, with the proper attitude, it will make your bond stronger.

Challenging experiences are not a prerequisite for developing a bond with another human, thankfully. There was the time, for instance, when Terra Firma, moored in Lima, Peru, was feeling abandoned because we had just accepted a work assignment in India. Out of the blue, when we were in Chennai, India, Carrie received an email from Gonzalo in Lima. "Why is your beautiful boat here with no one to look after her? Do you need any assistance?" Carrie responded, "Who are you? How did you find us?" "I am the Seven Seas Cruising Association ambassador in Peru," he replied, "and since you are also members I was able to acquire your email address." Upon our return to Peru, Gonzalo assisted us in so many ways that it would take volumes to describe them all. But the real treat was meeting his family, enjoying parties at his home, and being wined and dined at wonderful restaurants all over Lima. The sharing of the local adult beverage is also a great way to develop a bond, and with Gonzalo we downed many a Pisco, Peru's national drink. (By the way, Peruvian food is some of the best in the world. Visit Peru, if for no other reason than for the culinary experience.) Later that year, Gonzalo was named the Seven Seas Cruising Association Ambassador of the Year, a well-deserved honor. As Carrie stresses throughout the book, stay open to getting involved with locals.

For the next few years we wandered around South America with the goal of eventually reaching the southern tip. Bariloche, Argentina, in Northern Patagonia, was one of the stops on our way south. That is where we met Roxi. We first heard of Roxi from friends of hers in San Diego who told us to look her up if we ever got to Bariloche. Roxi, a retired aviator, had decided to make Bariloche her home, so we gave her a call, and after an 'interview,' we were invited to stay at her beautiful 'cabin' for a few weeks where we drank, hiked, ate wonderful Argentine beef, and helped Roxi part with some of her retirement savings through the game of Farkel (first time we ever played it for money). We returned six months later for more Farkel, food, and fun(ds). Yes, the Andes were beautiful, the lakes pristine, but long after the jagged mountain peaks and the sapphire blue of the mountain lakes had faded from the mind's eye, the friendships we had developed remained clear.

As with all things in life, change is inevitable, so in 2010 we sold the boat, our beloved Terra Firma — we had thought that we would live the rest of our lives with her — and readied ourselves for our next chapter.

Thinking it possible to settle down for a while — perhaps even a necessity — we bought a house in Arizona and did the normal stuff: remodeled the house, planted a garden, and tried to find our niche within the community. It was fun. To satisfy our wanderlust, we would jump into our 2003 Subaru — our version of the French Porsche (read on to find out about the French Porsche) — and road-trip our way through the western national parks. But the rest of the planet that we had not yet seen beckoned, so we made the bold decision to lease out our home for two years and go somewhere, anywhere. Just go. We devised a starting plan, and then our plan was simply to just wing it.

Oddly, the same thing happened to us this time as had occurred when we were on the boat. Our most cherished memories, the stories we recount most often, involved the people we met more than the places we visited. Let me give you a few examples, and if this doesn't whet your appetite for free-form travel, then you're hopeless.

Everything wonderful that's wrapped into the human genetic code — but with a quadruple dose of the crazy gene — is how best to describe Karine and her cohorts Arantxa and Marie. After spending three months wandering around Southeast Asia, it was time for us to head to Europe. First stop Perpignan, France. We wanted to settle in for a while, so we rented Karine's Airbnb apartment for a full month. The first event occurred about a week into our stay. We were sitting on our patio relaxing when Karine showed up and said, "Come on, we're going to Girona, Spain, for the flower festival!" So, we hopped into her circa-1989 Peugeot — the notorious French Porsche — and off to the psychedelic flower show we went for a Hunter S. Thompson Gonzo-style experience. A few days later, we were road-tripping again, this time to Banyuls and Collioure (on the Mediterranean coast) to have lunch with Arantxa, and then off wine tasting for the rest of the afternoon. A few days later, now fully recovered from the last road trip, we were back in the

French Porsche, this time off to Les Bains de St. Thomas, hot springs nestled in a remote area of the Pyrenees (my first experience wearing a speedo — eewww!). Then it was hiking through Orgue d'Ille Sur Tet ending with apero time (happy hour) at Karine's parents' home. A year later we returned, this time for only a week, and the craziness continued as if we had never left and, of course, back in the Porsche again for a road trip to Roses, Spain, a tourist town on the Mediterranean where Marie owned a flat. A wonderful two days of partying hard was had before we headed back to Perpignan. More memorable events ensued right up to the last day.

As I mentioned earlier, the sharing of potent imbibements is a great way to meet and bond with like-minded people. So, I'm sure it will come as no surprise that we are frequently found in wine bars, distilleries, and when in England, pubs. We met Jo on one such pub visit. Jo, the owner of The Corner House Pub in Cambridge, England — and in my opinion one of the finest pubs in the UK — adopted us while we were recovering from a not-so-pleasant Airbnb experience. We were to be in Cambridge for three days, and we tried to do the normal sightseeing things. After all, Cambridge is the home of Stephen Hawking's alma mater, but surprisingly we soon found ourselves drifting back to The Corner House for just one more pint and some of the best food in all of the UK. It just so happened that Jo's Mum (that's how they say Mom in the UK) was visiting from her home in Lesbos, Greece, to plan her son's upcoming wedding which would occur the following year in Lesbos. "Right then, why don't you two come to the wedding? You'll love my brother Royston and his fiancée Claire," Jo said. Carrie and I looked at each other, shrugged and replied, "OK!" We were simply following Travel Rule #1, about which you will soon learn. The following summer we met Roy and Claire, who welcomed us like we were part of the family. We were so fortunate to share so many experiences with so many wonderful people during the ten days we spent on Lesbos: Pints with Simon and Roy at the bar in the village of Skoutaros, an afternoon with Catherine at her hilltop home overlooking the Mediterranean, and the wedding to end all weddings. I also learned that the Brits are the royalty of partying. Even I was humbled by their drinking ability. Cheers!

The names of so many flood the memory: Georgina and her cats (UK), The Chase Pub (UK), Cvetelina (Bulgaria), our German 'girlfriends' Lilly and Annika (Guatemala), our Bolivian friend Victor (Guatemala), Martin and Blaga (Bulgaria), and countless sailing friends. The list seems endless. The stories could go on and on because they make me smile. I hope that one of the takeaways from my stories is that through travel you gain an insight into the lives of people from different lands and that when you make the effort the result is the gift of life long friendships that transcend political boundaries and diverse ideologies. That is why we travel.

Give Me Things That Don't Get Lost (Neil Young From 'Old Man')

Are we better people after 27 years spent mostly on the road, without ever establishing permanent roots? I would like to think so because it ain't easy leaving one's comfort zone. I think we're now better equipped to empathize and sympathize. We have a greater appreciation of this planet's beauty, its power, and its frailty. We have learned the joy of friends gained and the pain of friends lost. Borders mean nothing, we have learned, because people all over the world, for all their cultural, religious, and political differences, want and need the same things. We have found that laughter is the universal language and that time with people is what matters. It provides wonderful experiences if you let it.

If you're not sure that traveling is for you, this book will certainly whet your appetite and give you the confidence to give it a go. If you already have wanderlust or are experienced travelers, it will provide insights and tips that will make your travel more efficient and, most importantly, more fun. So, don't waste a second, jump on that magic carpet, and get out there and be happy!

Hike Drink Live Laugh (Apero Time)

Acknowledgements

It is impossible for me to thank Frank McCamley enough for the countless hours and heroic effort he put into reading and editing this book. He quietly endured my abusive relationship with pronouns and tenses and pushed past my complete lack of respect for the comma. By the way, Frank, I enjoyed the puns and banter, too. You are a saint. Thank you.

Special thanks to Sara Ahern who designed the awesome cover and who politely didn't burst into uncontrollable laughter when I showed her my attempts at covers. Sara, thank you for your professionalism and your friendship. I'm so happy that I was able to lure you into the yard all of those years ago with the promise of a paltry cheap scotch on the rocks.

Thank you to my super beta readers, Miriam Bruls and Jan Schwab, who read the book cover to cover and offered constructive suggestions and honest feedback. Also, an honorable mention to Carol Feldmann especially for her review of the Technology chapter.

Finally, many thanks to Pat for reminding me every few days to get off the couch and to go bathe and change my clothes, and for placing food and drink, especially coffee, within my reach. It just occurred to me that those acts of kindness may have been solely self-serving. Whatever your motivations, Sweetie, thank you.

Introduction

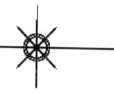

Carrie and Pat have been traveling for practically their entire lives, and obviously for all of their 27 years of marriage. This book shares the tips, strategies, and advice that they have acquired through their years of GlobeWandering, and relates many personal accounts of the good, the bad, and the ugly parts of travel. It's mostly about the good, though, and you can avoid the bad and the ugly with the knowledge you'll gain by reading this book.

The advice is intended for adventurous souls with an intense case of wanderlust but with only a modest travel budget. It is also intended for those who are unsure if GlobeWandering is within their ability. It is! Written from the perspective of traveling as a couple, its advice is pertinent to individuals as well. It is geared particularly for "grown-ups" or at least wanderers who prefer a bit of comfort. (I was going to use "adults," but do you know what the search engines pull up for "adult travel?" Oh, my.) Still, even if you are a solo backpacker who doesn't mind sleeping in dorms (only mentioned in passing in this book) and hitchhiking from town to town (not mentioned at all), there are valuable and unique tips that will prepare you for your journey, save you money, increase your comfort, and make your travels more enjoyable — possibly epic.

(Okay, be honest. Did you google "adult travel" before finishing that last paragraph?)

In the Transportation chapter, you'll hop on the fast track to finding inexpensive ways of getting around, including intercontinental airfare and transoceanic cruises, and how to ride public transportation as if you've been doing it all of your life. The Accommodations chapter will lay to rest your concerns about how to put an affordable roof over your head, even in notoriously expensive locales. The chapters on Money Matters, Travel Documents, and Insurance will provide a wealth of information ensuring that you are prepared for your trip and will set you on the golden path to saving money even before you leave.

The Technology chapter will get down and geeky with details of which electronics you should carry, with an in-depth look at the advantages of using a smartphone in foreign lands. The Gear chapter will shift the focus to items that can make traveling easier and less expensive too. Then, in the Guidebooks and Tourist Information chapter, you will be given not only recommendations for where to find the best information but a method for never missing an attraction, restaurant or curiosity that you want to see.

Additionally, since travel requires a certain disposition if you are going to have any fun at all, there is a chapter on Attitude. It covers pace and patience, and in it you will learn Travel Rule #1. It's the most important rule. That's why it's #1, and following Travel Rule #1 is what can make your trip truly epic.

Ready. Set. Go travel!

A Note from the Author

You will notice throughout the book snippets of stories from our travels. Pat and I co-author a travel blog called VinoHiking.com, and the excerpts come from there. We have written about our travels since 2005 when we retired. Some of the posts are pieces of insight, reflection, and occasional mayhem that you may find interesting and/or humorous to read. Additionally, Pat's photographs are stunning. Check out the Barcelona post to see what I mean.

Why VinoHiking? Well, this isn't a spoiler, but we like wine and we like hiking. Putting the two together just made sense to us. When we go for a hike, we take a bottle of wine and some tasty snacks. Once at our destination, usually a spot with a magnificent view, we sit down, relax, enjoy nature, or a park, or a village, and have our VinoLunch. Cheese and crackers, a handful of nuts, slices of apple, and a feisty Mourvedre are a lot more palatable than a peanut butter/barley/sawdust protein bar washed down with blue sports drink while trying to palpate a heart rate, just to turn around and head back down the mountain without even appreciating the view... I digress. Sorry.

So, as you read the book, when you come to a blog snippet, you can click on the caption below it (in the ebook version, of course) to see the post in its entirety, if you are so inclined, or you can visit our blog and simply wander through it at your convenience.

Hike Drink Live Laugh

VinoHiking.com

Attitude

"We checked in and asked the host about a grocery store and a restaurant. The town was about 4 km away, so she offered to drive us. We thanked her and gladly accepted, but what started as a simple grocery run soon turned into a full-day adventure.

Aldina, our host, Carlos, the guesthouse owner, and Pat and I went off toward town. Aldina asked, 'Would you like to see the fort? It has a great view. Then we can show you where to catch the bus to Setúbal where you might like to spend the day.' We thought that sounded like a nice plan and said as much. Besides, [as you'll learn later] Travel Rule #1 compelled it. We chatted along the way, asked each other about ourselves and about what was special to eat, drink, and see.

Aldina's opinion was spot on. The view from the fort was expansive. Below, we could see the river emptying into the ocean, the town of Setúbal on the coast, and green hills embracing cool valleys. Very pretty. Aldina led us into a small shop at the fort that sold hand-painted tiles. The artist wasn't there, but her English husband was. He showed us his wife's portfolio of custom-tile murals and individual pieces. She is a gifted artist, and he is quite the traveler, so we swapped stories for a bit.

*'Do you want to stop to try Muscatelo, the local wine
before we drop you at the bus stop?' asked Aldina. We
said yes. Shocking, I know, but who are we to not heed
Rule #1?"*

**The Start of a Full-Day Adventure in Palmela,
Portugal**

Attitude? What does that have to do with traveling on a
budget? Well, as it turns out... everything. You need to shift
gears, embrace patience, and put yourself out there.
Adopting a good travel attitude can not only save you money
but can open doors for you too.

Slow Down

Ok, you've set aside some time to "travel the world."
Excellent! Your goal is to see and do as much as you
possibly can on this beautiful blue marble. Whoa. Stop right
there... Seeing, but more importantly, experiencing a lot of a
little is infinitely more rewarding than seeing a little of a lot.
Traveling slowly is good for the soul and easy on the
pocketbook too.

Not surprisingly, if you spend more time at each destination,
you will need to take fewer planes, trains, or buses. That
helps a great deal in keeping the average daily burn-rate
down. The money not spent on transportation can go toward
something more exciting than six hours of staring out of a
bus window while scooting down the expressway. Have a
meal in a fancy restaurant instead. Go to a concert. Brave
the zip-lines. Intensely explore where you are. Walk
everywhere. Poke around the markets and shops. Picnic in
the parks. You will remember the place, not because of the
selfie that you took in front of the town's iconic sight but
because of the experiences you had while you were there.

Also, traveling slowly can make your accommodations less
expensive. When you book a place for a full week or a full
month, you will often receive a discount. Additionally, the
weekly or monthly discount may put renting an apartment, or
a place with access to a kitchen, within your budgetary
reach. I don't know about you, but I don't like to eat in a

restaurant for every meal. Cooking for yourself is a nice break from restaurants, and it saves money too, freeing up more of the daily budget for fun stuff. So, when you do go out, go ahead, order the foie gras!

Another reason to spend a week or more at a destination and not merely a night or two is that the pack-schlep-travel-schlep-unpack cycle gets tiresome. You wind up spending more of your time in transit than exploring or meeting people. I've heard it said that the journey is the destination, but honestly, I don't think that applies to planes or buses (maybe some trains, though). The destination is always more comfortable and relaxing, and inevitably more interesting.

Another thing about being in one place for an extended period is that it exposes you to the same people repeatedly — maybe your host, a shop owner, or a bartender. Let your inner extrovert out. Strike up a conversation, and who knows, you may learn things you wouldn't otherwise have discovered on your own. Take that person's advice and go see the recommended museum. Check out the sculptures in the park or try a local delicacy in a hard-to-find seafood shack. Then, the next time you two meet, you automatically have something to discuss. I love walking into a shop, restaurant, or bar in a foreign country and feeling like Norm from Cheers!

> *"Hue was a nice city and much smaller than Hanoi. We only had a day and a half to explore it, though, so we toured the Forbidden Palace and made sure we found a place that served Banh Khoai. Banh Khoai were called pancakes in English, but they were unlike any pancakes I had ever eaten. The woman who made them had a three-burner stove set up right on the sidewalk so passers-by could get a whiff of the addictive delights. Her father, who we think was a deaf mute, took the orders and delivered the pancakes and beers.*
>
> *To say he 'delivered beers' is an understatement. He set our four beers on the table and then produced a small plank of wood with a bolt sticking out near one end. He hooked the bolt over the lip of one of the bottle caps, made*

23

some silent martial arts moves, and then gave the plank a karate whack. The cap and the plank flew into the air and then he caught the plank in one fluid motion. He gave it a few ninja twirls and then attacked the remaining three beers in a similar fashion. We all smiled and clapped. His face filled with a smile, and he gave us a big thumbs-up.

Our visit to Hue was very short. The next day we had to catch a 1:30pm bus to Hoi An, so we had just enough time to do a little computer work, find an ATM, and have lunch. Take a guess at what we chose for lunch! Both daughter and father greeted us like regulars as we walked into their restaurant for more of those wonderfully crispy, peanut-sauce-covered, pork- and shrimp-filled pancakes of bliss. What a great last taste to have in your mouth as you leave Hue."

Feeling like Norm in Hue, Vietnam

Have a Plan

Yes, have a plan, but don't over-plan. If you're going abroad for more than a couple of weeks, don't plan every single little detail. When Pat and I get ready to go away, generally for six months or more at a time, I book one-way transportation to the first destination and reserve the first accommodation. That's it. I do the rest of the planning on the road, as needed. Pat and I like to call it "free-form" travel, although others might frown and call it "winging it" in a not-so-complimentary tone. Vive la différence!

"'You know it's almost September, right?' Pat asked me. I guess I had a vague notion. 'Where are we going next?' he continued. That was a good question. We wanted to see so much — Moldova, Hungary, Croatia, and Slovenia, before heading back into Italy and checking out Venice, then to France for Nice and Montpellier. We also knew that we wanted to spend a month tooling around the French countryside searching for wine. We hear they make some good stuff. We also wanted to spend at least a week in Perpignan. Everything else needed to fit into the next two months. Why were we still in Romania?

24

Scratch Moldova. It was in the wrong direction. I worked backwards from our drop-dead date of Nov 5th, the day on which we needed to be in Barcelona to board the ship. Did I mention we were taking a cruise ship back to the States? No? Well, that's another story for another post. We could fit Budapest, Zagreb, and Ljubljana into a short period since they aren't too far apart. The rest of Hungary, Croatia, and Slovenia would need to wait for another time."

Free-Form Traveling

Obviously, free-form travel lets you go wherever you please when you please. Have you wound up somewhere amazing and wanted to spend more time there? Do it. Have you landed somewhere that you really couldn't stand? Leave. Was there a concert or festival that you absolutely had to see taking place in a town that you'd never even heard of? No problem, go, but if you have all of your transportation and your accommodation for your entire trip reserved in advance, you're far less likely to go to the concert or festival because it's a hassle, and sometimes it costs money to cancel a reservation.

"We had booked four nights in Melnik, even though people had told us that one day was all we needed. It was a town of only 385 people after all. I guess we all need different things. We extended our stay to an entire week because we were having such an enjoyable time. Our room had a comfortable bed and A/C, and the town's topography, museums, and ruins were interesting. Best of all, Melnik was awash in wonderful wine!"

Adjusting Plans on the Fly in Melnik, Bulgaria

So, if you go free-form, can you get shut out of places? Yes, of course, but do you really want to go somewhere when it's packed with tourists? Maybe you have a bucket list event that you want to attend regardless of the crowds. In that case, be sure to book your tickets, transportation, and room in advance for that event. Just let your itinerary, before and after, develop on its own.

Other reasons to keep your plans flexible might include meeting people with whom you'd like to travel. There is power in numbers. Sharing transportation and accommodation are both money-saving moves. Did you make friends with a local family? They might invite you to spend some time in their home. Staying with a local family can be a very special experience, and free accommodation is a nice bonus! Or maybe you caught a cold and aren't up to traveling until you feel better. Or perhaps the weather is inclement where you were considering going next. The reasons to do your planning on the road are countless.

Travel Rule #1

This is the biggie, and it's really simple. If a local invites you to do something or go somewhere (unless you are absolutely certain that bodily harm will come of it), say yes! My fondest travel memories are the experiences that happened as a result of Travel Rule #1.

Travel Rule #1 came to be because when Pat and I were neophyte travelers, we were on a small Fijian island and were invited to a professor's home for tea. We thanked him and politely declined. Why? I don't know. It's not like we thought he was a cannibal who was going to throw us into a bubbling people-sized stock pot with carrots and onions. Nor did we think he was going to poison us and steal all of our cash (which was in our wallets, in our back pockets. Neophytes, I tell you). Later that evening, a friend who was traveling with us recounted her afternoon of sipping tea and chatting with presumably that same professor. It sounded magical, and we quietly scolded ourselves for not having accepted the invitation. Right then is when Travel Rule #1 was born and put into effect with the stipulation that it can never be overruled.

You can't plan for these experiences, but when they happen, they are the cherries on the travel sundae. When a local invites you to do something, it's because they think you will enjoy it. Take the blog excerpt at the beginning of this chapter, for example. We wanted groceries and a restaurant. What we got instead was an incredibly memorable day with two very interesting, fun, and kind people. It started with the view from the fort, then a taste of Moscatel, then heaping plates of fish and pitchers of wine. Eventually, we wound up at a bar to watch a soccer match, eat choco frito (fried cuttlefish), and drink more wine. We laughed and talked and learned about each other's philosophies and about life in general. You can't pay for stuff like that, but you can miss out if you don't follow Travel Rule #1.

I can go on and on with examples, but I will just mention a few briefly with links to the corresponding blog posts if you are interested in reading more. In Melnik, Bulgaria, a restaurant owner took the time to chat with us and, upon learning of our love of wine, insisted on taking us to a winery where we met the winemaker and sampled outstanding wines. In Armagh, Ireland, my high school English teacher's hometown, we met a friendly pub owner with plenty of tales to tell about my teacher's family. In Ljubljana, Slovenia, we savored an authentic Slovenian dinner with people whom we had met in Bulgaria while they were road-tripping on their Harley Davidson. Since then, they have visited the States, and we were able to return the favor. In Thailand and Vietnam, we hooked up with sailing friends to tour together. And I have to mention the winemaker in Thuir, France, who drove us way out to his vineyard in the foothills of the Pyrenees to "see his office."

For me, these unexpected, one-of-a-kind experiences are the gold nuggets. Sure, Machu Picchu was great. Angkor Wat was mind-blowing. The Colosseum was astounding. But the unique encounters are why I travel, and they all happened because of following Travel Rule #1. By the way, if you must know, I still kick myself for not sitting down to tea with the professor in Fiji. It's a regret I'll have for the rest of my life, but good came from it in that Travel Rule #1 was born.

The Language Barrier

Though mingling with people spices your travels, often these people speak a different language. It's okay not to understand their language. If you are a North American like I am, you probably speak only one language fluently, maybe two at most, unless you are some sort of linguistic savant.

So, how do you get by in a country with a different language? What about a country with an entirely different alphabet? Well, it isn't as terrifying as it sounds. All you need is a good attitude, and anyone can afford one of those.

A little study and a lot of patience will go a long way toward making people want to interact with you and help you, and brushing up on your charades skills won't hurt either. For starters, learn a few words in the country's native tongue. "Hello," "thank you," "yes," and "no" are great places to start. When you have those words down, add a few more, such as "goodbye," "good morning," "good night," and "beer," if you like. "Toilet" is also a good word to know if you plan to use "beer." Just attempting to speak a few words can make people much more receptive, and you may even find that they do know how to speak a bit of English after all. In Spanish-speaking countries, I'm no longer shy about mutilating the language. Many times, I'll get through an awkward sentence or two, and that's about the time the other person decides that they know more English than I know Spanish, so we continue in English.

When you get super-stuck but need to communicate a question or a request that has to be completely understood, look for a young person. Schools all around the world are teaching English, and there's always a high school kid tickled to show off his or her proficiency. If you still can't find someone to translate, resort to the Google Translate app (detailed in the Technology chapter). It's less personal and a bit clunky, but it beats accidentally proposing marriage to the shopkeeper's twelve-year-old daughter when you are trying to mime that you want to rent a motorbike to ride on rough terrain.

"Once we arrived in Septemvri, we needed to purchase tickets for the next leg to Sofia. Finding the ticket office was no problem. Buying tickets, however, was a huge problem. You see, for some reason, the ticket agent, whom we had seen selling tickets to Bulgarian customers, refused to understand that we wanted the same tickets. Instead, she kept directing us to the train platform without a ticket. We finally found a helpful Bulgarian who spoke English and told him of our predicament. He

went directly up to the ticket window and told her to sell us two train tickets to Sofia. She wasn't happy, but she obliged. What a rectal orifice! (I was going to use a more efficient expression, but Carrie didn't like it.)"

Finding a Translator at the Train Station in Septemvri, Bulgaria

And, remember, everyone speaks "body language." Be conscious of the impression you are giving. Crossed-arms and a scowl mean the same thing everywhere — don't bother me, go away. On the other hand, an open posture and a smile indicate that you are approachable and amenable to interaction. Looking lost and befuddled is another effective way to ask for help without saying a word. Practice in a mirror. No, not really, but send a video if you do!

Customs and Cultural Differences

No one likes to make their first impression a cultural faux pas. Customs, traditions, and social norms change from country to country and even from region to region within a country. In India, touching someone or food with your left hand is a no-no, and men shouldn't touch women at all, not even with a handshake. In Japan, sticking your chopsticks vertically into your food can draw cross looks from other patrons in a restaurant and entering a Buddhist temple while wearing shorts, shoes, and with uncovered shoulders is considered very disrespectful.

So, how do you know who you may or may not touch and with which hand? How do you know what the proper attire is or what's appropriate dining etiquette? Read your guidebook. Do an internet search for proper etiquette while traveling in Country X. Ask your hosts what they have noticed other travelers doing that is inappropriate. You don't want to be "that guy" or "that gal."

But even after preemptive study, you will unintentionally offend at some point in your travels. It happens, so just learn from your mistake and apologize profusely. Some unwritten rules can be subtle. For instance, imagine you are finally getting comfortable speaking a little Spanish when you go into a market to buy some eggs. You proudly ask the man behind the counter, "¿Tienes huevos?" Well, you just asked him if he has balls, and one of two things will happen next. He will become irate and start yelling at you in Spanish, using words you are unlikely to know. Or, as I found out, he may burst into laughter and explain to you what you have said and give you the proper phrase, "¿Hay huevos?" Are there eggs? Live and learn!

Money Matters

"All roads lead to Liberia. We went through this city three times while visiting Costa Rica. Liberia wasn't bad for a hub-city, and we had some tasty crave-quenching Chinese food there. We were shocked, however, when the bill for the meal came to over $4,000. It wasn't that good! Well, it wasn't really $4,000 either. The exchange rate was $517 colones to the dollar. Pat thought we had hit the jackpot when he asked the ATM for $200US and got over $100,000 colones in return. Woohoo! Look at all that dough. We laid it out on the bed and rolled around in it for a while."

Hitting the Jackpot in Liberia, Costa Rica

Having a budget and sticking to it is vital to achieving successful, stress-free travel, and using the right credit cards, debit cards, and currency exchange methods can keep money in your pocket.

The Budget

One of the very first steps you should take in planning your great adventure is determining your budget. This isn't exciting stuff, but it's crucial. To keep the math simple, let's assume that your trip will last one year. You will need to know your expected income and fixed expenses for the year. Whatever is left over is your travel budget.

I'm sure you are curious about what our travel budget is. I'll tell you now that it's $100/day, and on that amount, Pat and I travel comfortably. One hundred dollars per day is how much we have for absolutely everything — international transportation, accommodations, rental cars, trains, food, booze, tours, corn pads... absolutely everything. If you follow our money-saving strategies and tips, you can travel comfortably too, possibly for even less (the booze portion of our budget is larger than average).

Income

First, you need to figure all of your sources of income. Have you been building a travel kitty for this excursion over the past couple of years? That counts as income. Are you renting out your primary residence while you're away? The rent counts as income. Do you receive social security and/or a pension? Dividends and/or interest? Book royalties (I'm hoping I will)? Do you have a benevolent aunt who sends you a generous monthly stipend (I wish I did)? Those all count too.

Pat is the money person in our family, and he uses a spreadsheet to calculate our budget. Depending on what you are comfortable doing, you can create your own spreadsheet, find a freebie on the internet, use Quicken, or go old school and write it out by hand. However you choose to do it, add up all of your income for the year and compute the total. I hope it's a nice big number.

Fixed Expenses

Now, you need to add up all of your fixed expenses for the year. This isn't nearly as fun as adding up income, but it's a necessary evil. Fixed expenses may include home, auto, life, health, or other insurance obligations. Also included are debts (mortgage, student loan, a line of credit, etc.), out-of-pocket medical/dental expenses, property taxes, and the cost of tax return preparation. Additionally, don't forget new expenses that you may have while traveling, such as Amazon Prime, Kindle Unlimited, Tunnelbear VPN, and a web-hosting service (for your new travel blog!). If you are renting your home out, remember the property manager's fee and the amount needed for property maintenance.

Calculate your annual fixed expenses. I hope this is a small number.

Travel Budget

Now for the moment of truth. Take your annual fixed expenses and subtract them from your annual income. It's okay. You can open your eyes. This is your travel budget for your year of travel. Now divide it by 365 and you'll know what you can spend per day... on average.

"On average" is an important concept. You don't have to hit your daily budget every single day. Sometimes you'll have no choice but to go over. When you buy intercontinental transportation, it will strain the budget. The trick is to absorb big purchases over time by staying under budget as much as possible until you are back on track.

Tracking Expenses

Figuring out your travel budget allowance is only useful if you diligently track your expenses. Again, Pat is the money guy, and he religiously records all of our expenses in a spreadsheet. At the end of each week, he tabulates how much over budget or under budget we are for the week, and where we stand since the beginning of the trip. If it turns out that we are over budget, we'll try to be "good" during the next week. We also keep in the back of our minds any large purchases that may be on the horizon, such as airline or cruise ship tickets. We try to "behave" in the weeks leading up to purchasing intercontinental transportation so that we stay in, or near, the black when we make the purchase.

> *"After many months of talking about a plan to fly off to Southeast Asia, we were finally committed. Not to a mental institution like some of you probably think, but to the trip itself. With my hands sweating as I plugged in the final digits of the credit card number I double-, triple-, and quadruple-checked the date and destination, and*

then bought our tickets to Kuala Lumpur, Malaysia, online. It was time to paint or get off the pot."

Making a Large Purchase to Get the Trip Rolling

Pat uses Quicken in addition to the spreadsheet to track our income and expenses. Quicken is a program that provides a snapshot of your financial situation. With it, Pat can directly import credit card transactions from the credit card companies into the database and not have to type it all in by hand. Once he has imported the transactions, he reviews each one, first to make sure that we made the charge, and second, to verify that the category is correct. Purchases are automatically categorized by Quicken, or a category can be selected manually. Categories may include groceries, gifts, gas, etc., and they can also be made quite specific to aid in statistical analysis, if you're into that sort of thing. Pat can also flag the category as tax-deductible so that expenses in that category will come up in a tax report. He downloads the bank statements and goes through the same process of reviewing each transaction. At the end of the year, Quicken makes it easy for Pat to create a report that our tax guy can use to prepare our taxes. Another feature of Quicken is that it can create a budget. Pat is partial to his spreadsheet, so he has not used this feature, but you might find it useful.

Whether you use a spreadsheet, or Quicken, or both, the important thing to know is what your daily burn-rate is and to stick to your budget. Also, be sure to frequently back up either or both to the cloud.

Credit Cards

Credit cards are a convenient method of payment and make currency conversion seamless. In fact, credit cards often give the best currency exchange rates. They present a couple of issues, however. First of all, some parts of the world don't widely accept credit cards, only cash. Another annoyance is the foreign transaction fee. When you charge a meal, or room, or tickets to your credit card in a foreign country, your credit card company charges you a foreign transaction fee, usually around 3%. Sounds small, right?

Well, look at it this way. If your budget is $100/day and you stay exactly on budget and charge all of your purchases to your credit card, that's $3/day. Still sounds small, right? It's not. If your trip is one year, 365 days, that's almost $1,100 being spent on nothing. Think of all the other things you could do with that amount of money!

Before you run screaming from the room to jam your credit cards into the shredder, there's good news. Some credit card companies offer cards with "no foreign transaction fee" and those cards are easy to find. Heck, you might already have one in your wallet. Just check your card's terms and conditions. If you don't have such a card, search the internet for "best no foreign fee cards." Each year, many independent review sites make a list of the top ten. While you are comparing cards, also look for rental car insurance (if you plan to rent cars internationally) and see if they offer any trip insurance.

Cards with airline or hotel rewards points are worth considering too. I've had miserable luck with redeeming airline miles, but I love the Chase Marriott card. The card has no foreign transaction fees, and it includes international rental car insurance and some trip insurance (trip delay, baggage delay/loss). Although the card has an annual fee, you receive a free night at a Marriott hotel. Okay, it's more of a prepaid night than a free night, but any excuse to spend a night in a Marriott is fine with me! By using this card for almost all purchases, we have stayed in some amazing Marriotts around the world on rewards points.

> "After spending six weeks sleeping in dorm rooms,
> miniscule private rooms with a shared-bath, party-
> hostels, nice hostels, uncomfortable bus seats, and a tent,
> it was time to treat ourselves. First of all, we opted to fly
> from Ushuaia to Buenos Aires instead of spending over
> 40 hours on yet another bus. Second, we burned some of
> the Marriott points that we had earned while w-w-
> working in the States last year and spent four heavenly

nights in the downtown hotel. They greeted us as if we
were royalty even though it must have appeared, and
smelled, like we were stall-muckers for the royal pony
brigade."

In Our Early GlobeWandering Days, Living the
Good Life on Points

An important point to remember about credit cards is that
credit card companies take fraud seriously. If they see that
your card is being used outside of your usual locations, they
will shut your card down unless you alert them in advance.
So, before traveling, call your credit card company, or go
online and let them know where you'll be visiting and when
you'll be there. Don't worry if you don't know your entire
itinerary. Just let the credit card company know before you
enter a new country.

Another piece of credit card advice is that you should take a
minimum of two credit cards with you. Being unexpectedly
shut down can be extremely inconvenient. You certainly
don't want to be standing at the ticket counter in a train
station when it happens, especially if you don't have an
alternate card. When we were in Ensenada, Mexico, many
years ago, our card was shut down when we were trying to
buy groceries. No problem. We simply paid with another
card and then contacted our credit card company as soon as
we could. It turned out that the card that had been shut down
had been "skimmed." The account information had been
read from our credit card strip and then resold to someone
who had made a new card... in Zimbabwe. The credit card
company was wise, although a little slow, to recognize that it
was unlikely that while we were buying groceries in Mexico
(where we had alerted them we would be) that we were
simultaneously splurging on a used car and other items in
Zimbabwe. But that was back in the days of magnetic strips.
Aren't chip cards completely secure? Unfortunately, not.
Now a device called a "shimmer" exists which makes
stealing the account info from a chip card possible.

Skimmers and, even more so, shimmers are difficult to
detect. Skimmers look like a regular credit card reader and
are attached to things such as the card slots on ticket kiosks

36

and pay-at-the-pump machines. Worse yet, shimmers can't even be seen since they are inserted inside the machine. The best advice I can give you is to check your credit card transactions online regularly and to contact your credit card company if you notice any transactions that you didn't make.

One more point. If you are ever asked if you want to pay in the local currency or your home currency, always pay in the local currency. Some cards charge an extra fee for the convenience of converting the bill into your home currency.

Debit Cards

In order to play the ATM slot machine, you will need a debit card. In countries where cash is king and credit card-accepting businesses are scarce, you will use ATMs often to obtain the local currency. As with credit cards, notify your bank of your travel plans, or they may shut down your debit card and possibly deny you online access to your account if they notice activity out of your usual area.

Of course, drawbacks exist. The biggest drawback is the dreaded ATM fee. Your US bank may charge as much as $5 (Wells Fargo, for one) each time you use an ATM that either isn't theirs or isn't in their network. That stinks. But wait, there's more. The bank in the foreign country may also charge $3 or so. That's eight bucks. Ouch! When looked at as a percentage, things can get ugly in a hurry since foreign banks usually limit you to how much you can withdraw from an ATM at a time, regardless of what your bank allows you to withdraw. A $200 limit is common (that works out to a 4% fee), but we have come across a limit as low as $100 (8% fee). Don't even consider withdrawing less than $200 unless it is a life-or-death emergency.

On top of ATM fees, debit cards may also have 2-3% foreign transaction fees. So, if you withdraw $200, as much as $14 can go to fees. Fees aren't food or fun. Who wants to spend travel dollars on that? Indulge me if you will, or you can skip to the next paragraph if numbers make your eyes roll to the back of your head. Assume $200 is two days' worth of your budget. In this case, $7/day goes toward ATM and transaction fees. If you use only ATMs during your year-long trip, you may spend over $2,500 in fees. Wow!

Fortunately, friends of ours told us about the Charles Schwab personal checking account and debit card. It has no foreign transaction fees and no ATM fees on either end, neither on Schwab's end nor on the foreign bank's. If the foreign bank does have an ATM fee, Schwab picks it up. Boy, am I glad that we have friends who share great tips like this! Maybe we should send them a fruit basket, or a Lamborghini, or something. If they weren't currently sailing somewhere in the middle of the Indian Ocean, we would.

If you don't want to change banks or open a new account, go visit your personal banker. If you have been a good customer for many years, he or she may make a provision to reverse the out-of-network ATM fee. It won't eliminate the foreign bank's ATM fee nor the foreign transaction fee if there is one, but it's worth checking into.

Unfortunately, as with credit cards, skimmers and shimmers can be used to hack your debit card too, and that's a big deal. For one thing, most people have only one personal checking account. So, if your checking account is hacked and someone swipes all of your funds, you are SOL. DO NOT put your entire travel kitty into your checking account that can be accessed with your debit card. Instead, keep that money in a savings account, or a brokerage account, and move small amounts into the checking account when you plan to make a withdrawal. Also, when using the ATM, make sure there are no prying eyes trying to heist your PIN. One of us always keeps an eye on the people nearby while the other uses the machine.

What if you find yourself in a situation where you are in one country and then travel to a new country that uses a different currency? Okay, that's not so odd, but if you are traveling by bus, bear in mind that buses don't stop at the nearest ATM once they cross the border. And, to compound matters, your destination might still be quite a few hours down the road. So, when the bus stops for a lunch-break, you can't count on your credit cards being accepted. Sure, you can pack your own bag-lunch, but your beer will be tepid. Bleh.

Couldn't you just go to a bank before boarding the bus and withdraw some cash in the next country's currency with a no-fee ATM card? Good thinking! Many times, yes. Unfortunately, you may not actually be able to do it at the ATM. Instead, you may need to go inside the bank during banking hours (watch out for holidays, short weekend hours, and mid-day closures). Most importantly, take your passport with you! We were in Saranda, Albania, and walked a few miles into town, down a respectable hill, to withdraw euros from an ATM. Our hosts told us it was possible. Well, it is, unless you aren't from Albania or a euro-using country. We had to go into the bank and present our passports, which were not so conveniently, but very securely, stowed inside our money belts and hidden back at the apartment. Our day instantly turned into a long, hot, grumpy one. Remember our pain, and take your passport with you.

One more tip on debit cards. If you are traveling with your spouse or partner and that person is on the checking account too, see if it is possible to be issued debit cards with different numbers. If one card is lost or stolen, you may be able to cancel the lost/stolen one and still be able to use the other card. Check with your bank.

Speaking of losing a debit card, we nearly lost one in Santiago, Chile. A little confused about how the ATM machine operated, we eventually coaxed it into giving us some cash. When it spat out the money, the bills seemed to be of enormous denominations, and we were concerned about being able to break them (They weren't. We were both doing poor mental math.). While we were standing in line for a teller so that we could (unnecessarily) break the bills, a little old woman tapped Pat on the shoulder and then started shaking her finger at him and scolding him in Spanish. He'd left his ATM card in the machine. She returned the card to him and then turned and left in a huff before he could even thank her. I'm surprised she didn't whack him on the back of the head for good measure. Since then, we have the "count to three" rule: cash, card, receipt. Count each one, and if you reach three, you're good.

Cash and Currency Exchange

At this point, you're probably thinking that the best course of action is to take as many greenbacks with you as you can and avoid all the credit card and debit card fees. Right? Well, how much are you willing to put into your money belt? $500? $1,000? $10,000? ($10,000 is usually the limit before you need to declare your cash when you go through customs.) I know for a fact that $500 in twenty-dollar bills and smaller makes a money belt pretty thick. In the past, Pat and I carried a lot of cash before ATMs and credit card acceptance became prevalent, but I can't imagine trying to stuff $10,000 into a money belt. That's a minimum of 100 bills!

Logistically, it would be difficult to stow more than two or three weeks' worth of cash in your money belt before you start looking as if you're trying to conceal an angry puffer fish under your clothes. With two people traveling together, that's one month to six weeks of your travel budget. It may be enough for a short trip, but I'd certainly be uncomfortable with that much cash on me for fear of loss or theft, and I certainly don't plan to sleep with my money belt on, do you?

Regarding the cash itself, the bills need to be new and crisp, especially $50 and $100 bills. Large bills with even the slightest blemish can be extremely difficult to spend or exchange. Shopkeepers and money-changers are always on the lookout for counterfeit bills and often treat any bill that isn't perfect as counterfeit. So, be careful when you put them into your money belt that you don't crease them or bend the corners.

Now, if you are in a country that officially, or otherwise, accepts the dollar, you and your travel companion are all set, at least for a month or so. Countries where the dollar is welcome include Cambodia, Panama, the Bahamas, Ethiopia, Turks and Caicos, Zimbabwe, El Salvador, Ecuador, Palau, Greece, Belize, and the British Virgin Islands.

If you're not in a country where you can directly spend your US dollars, however, you will need to exchange dollars for the local currency. Well, now you're back in the same boat as using a credit card with a foreign transaction fee. The currency exchange shops are going to charge an exchange fee, even if they claim to be "commission-free," to turn your dollars into their whatevers. Watch the money-changers carefully, and know what the current exchange rate should be. Don't be embarrassed to take your calculator out to check the conversion, and double-count the bills handed to you in front of the money-changer. Once you walk away, whatever you got is what you have.

Sometimes you find money-changers right at the border. If you are crossing by bus, the bus will make two stops, one stop to check out of the country you are leaving and another to check into the next country and to clear customs. Money-changers often lurk there hoping to rip-off unsuspecting tourists by charging an unfair exchange fee or to flat-out short-change them. Use these sketchy con-artists as a last resort. Exchange as little as possible, and know the exchange rate ahead of time. If you can't do the math in your head, use your calculator. Frankly, some of the exchange rates are challenging to convert in your head. Also, have the cash you want to exchange separated from the rest of your stash. You don't want to show these guys your entire wad. Finally, count the money twice while you still have the money-changer in front of you.

A last note on cash. when you exchange it for the local currency, be mindful of how long you will be in that country and needing its currency. If you wind up with a bunch of Lao kip on the day you plan to cross into Thailand, you'll need to exchange your kip for Thai baht and, of course, you'll incur yet another exchange fee. Pat is a master at estimating how much cash to get. We have never been stuck with enough to even concern ourselves with converting it, so we usually keep the leftover cash as souvenirs.

Taking Care of Business

It would be nice if leaving the US would somehow suspend all of your bills back home. Unfortunately, it doesn't. You may still need to pay insurance premiums, debt servicing, or expenses for unexpected maintenance on your home.

What's more, it's not as if you can write a check and pop it in the mail and expect it to arrive in a timely fashion.

To pay recurring and non-recurring bills, Pat uses the Bill Pay feature of the Schwab personal checking account. Most banks, if not all, have this feature, but some may charge for this pleasure. For the credit cards, Pat has each one linked to a personal checking account and he can use the credit   ฯ schedule a payment to occur on a date he

handling all of your finances online, set it before your trip and practice. Pat says it's ve him, but I seem to recall a little cursing at y accessing your accounts while using a the Technology chapter), too. Better yet, support at your bank, and tell them that VPN while accessing your account, and g so won't trip their fraud system. We had a ce with Wells Fargo completely shutting t while were in England, and we are e reason was the VPN. Long story short: done unless we went into a bank branch. re aren't any Wells Fargo branches in onger bank with Wells Fargo. The end.

Visa-vis Travel Documents

"'Americano! Americano!' That was the cry from the Bolivian immigration official as he caught a glimpse of our passports. It was as if the nation was on high alert. Three officials were needed to issue our visas and take our money. We were the only US citizens on the bus, which did not endear us to the rest of the passengers, since our immigration processing took so much longer than, say, our Canadian friends'.

Having survived the border crossing and thwarted an attempt at extorting $50 from us, we arrived at the other end of Lake Titicaca in the town of Copacabana."

Obtaining a Visa on Arrival in Bolivia - Fun Times

Everyone knows that you need a passport to travel to other countries, but occasionally you need more than that. Sometimes you need a visa or even a record of your vaccinations. Travel documents aren't the most enthralling subject, but you don't want any inconvenient surprises at a border-crossing, do you, so let's get started.

Passport (US)
If you have the travel bug, it's time to apply for your passport, or if you already have a passport, it's time to check

its expiration date and how full it is. Many countries require that your passport be valid for six to nine months after your entry date, and countries issuing visas may require up to two blank pages in your passport. Countries that do not require visas generally keep the immigration stamps (entry and exit) to half of a passport page, but if you run into a cantankerous official, he can smudge up a whole page if he's in a particularly surly mood. Make sure there is room in your passport for the expected visas and stamps (including a little extra room for the efforts of a few grumpy officials) and that your passport's expiration date is far enough in the future.

When applying for your first US passport or renewing your passport, you will need the following items and useful information:

Application Form
The form is available online at travel.state.gov. You can fill it out online and then print it, or you can print it and complete it by hand. For first-time applicants and those who need to renew passports that expired more than 15 years ago, use form DS-11. Otherwise, use form DS-82. Notice at the top of either form that there are checkboxes for US Passport Book, US Passport Card, and Both. If you plan to travel outside of North America (USA, Canada, Mexico), you will need a US Passport Book. You also need to select whether you want a regular book or a large book. Get the large book since you can no longer add pages to a US passport.

Proof of US Citizenship
If you are renewing your passport, you can submit your old passport as proof of citizenship, as long as it was issued when you were at least 16 years old. If you are a first-time applicant, you need to submit another form of proof of US citizenship, typically a certified birth certificate. Whatever proof of citizenship you supply, you also need to provide a photocopy of the front, and the back too, if there is information on both sides. If you do provide a birth certificate, it must include your full name, your date and place of birth, your sex, the date on which the birth record was filed, the seal or other certification of the official custodian of such records (state, county, or city/town office),

and the full names of your parent(s). The original will be sent back to you separately from your passport.

Proof of Identity
This is not needed for the renewal of a passport that expired fewer than 15 years ago. If you are applying for your first passport or renewing one that expired more than 15 years ago, you need to present proof of identity. Acceptable forms of identification include a driver's license (not a temporary or learner's license), a Certificate of Naturalization, a Certificate of Citizenship, a military identification document, or a federal, state, or municipal government employee identification card. The identification document must have your photo and signature. Temporary or altered documents are not acceptable. Also, you must provide a photocopy of the front and back of your proof of identity.

Color Photograph
You know what this is. It's the ugliest photo you've ever seen of yourself. It is the bad-hair-day photo that graces your passport for ten full years. Getting that ghastly image is easy, though, you can go to most drugstores, office supply stores, membership warehouses, or Walmart to have your passport photo taken. You can also take your own photo and print it at home on photo-quality paper. To make things easy, there are many websites that help you adjust your photo to the proper dimensions and give you other pointers regarding facial expression, background color, lighting, etc. One website that works well is: www.persofoto.com. Although you need to submit only one color photo with your passport application, you should print extras if you plan to visit countries that require visas.

Fees
Look up the current fees at travel.state.gov when you are making your application. They change from time to time, and there may be different fees depending on whether you need the process expedited or if the application is for a minor. Also, make sure you are aware of the method of payment required by the facility that is processing your application. Some take cash, some do not. Some take credit cards or

checks, others don't. Others may even take your firstborn child, but I'd avoid those facilities. It's your call, though.

Submitting the Application

Renewals are sent in by mail. First-time applicants, however, and those with passports that expired more than 15 years ago, must submit the application in person to a designated acceptance agent, in other words, a clerk of a federal or state court of record or a judge or clerk of a probate court accepting applications, a designated municipal or county official, a designated postal employee at an authorized post office, an agent at a passport agency, or a U.S. consular official at a U.S. Embassy or Consulate, if abroad. To find the nearest acceptance facility, visit travel.state.gov or contact the National Passport Information Center at 1-877-487-2778.

Processing Time

Routine processing time is four to six weeks. On the other hand, expedited processing time is two to three weeks and costs an additional $60. If you use the expedited service, you send the application to a different address which is listed on the application form. In case of emergency, it may be possible to have your passport expedited at an agency in only eight business days.

"Well, you know how the best-laid plans often go. Our bus stopped in the middle of almost nowhere when it encountered a long line of parked vehicles. After a couple of minutes, the bus turned around, shifted into reverse gear and drove backwards down the side of the road intended for oncoming traffic to the front of the line of cars nearly a mile away. At that point, we were told that there was a miners' strike and that they had blocked the road with a mound of rocks and dirt. If we wanted to continue to Tumbes, the bus driver would get our bags out, return a couple dollars of our bus fare and wish us good luck.

We didn't have a choice since we had already booked a flight to Lima out of Tumbes for that night. So off we went in a state of confusion with our backpacks on our backs to cross a tense picket line. On the other side of the picket line, a missionary and his assistant took pity on us and helped us get a collectivo (shared taxi), at an inflated rate due to the strike, into the next town where we could catch a bus to Huaquillas, Ecuador. There were no direct INTERNATIONAL buses to Tumbes, Peru. Drag! Fortunately, we managed to catch a bus fairly quickly, and just as quickly we zoomed past the Ecuadorian immigration office. When we figured out what had happened, we jumped off the bus, with the missionary still assisting us, and hailed a taxi to take us back to the immigration office. Now, with properly stamped passports, we taxied to the Peruvian border. What a zoo! At the border, the missionary made arrangements with a Peruvian taxi driver to take all of us to the Peruano immigration office, then to drop us off at the airport and finally to take him and his helper to Tumbes proper."

Making Sure Our Passports Were Properly Stamped

Passport (Dual-Citizenship)

Pat is in the enviable position of having both US and French citizenships and holds a passport for each country. It wasn't easy for him to apply for and obtain a French passport, but it was well worth the effort. It took time. He had to fill out forms in French, and although Pat is fluent in French, filling out forms required looking up words and phrases and, as you well know, speaking in a second language is quite different from writing in one. He had to request a new copy of his birth certificate from the city in France where he was born, in French of course. Once the forms were completed and the birth certificate was received, a face-to-face interview was conducted at the Consulat Général de France in Los Angeles, and then the whole package, plus about $100 for the passport, was sent off to France for approval. Upon approval, the passport was issued and sent to the nearest French address in the US, the honorary French consulate in Phoenix in this case, and then it had to be picked up in person. At least we didn't have to drive out to LA again.

Should you go through the hassle? Absolutely, especially if you can get a passport from a Schengen country (see the More on Visas section below). The first major benefit is that you don't need to worry one bit about how long you stay in the Schengen region when you travel on a European passport. For most non-European passport holders traveling in Europe for longer than three months, the Schengen region is a royal pain in the patootie. You need to keep track of how many days you've spent in the past 180 in Schengen countries, and then you are allowed only 90 days in that period. Pat kept threatening to leave me in Romania (non-Schengen) so that he could start enjoying some fine French Bordeaux wines (Schengen).

Another benefit to traveling on a European passport has to do with visas. Some countries require visas for US citizens but not Europeans. Take Bolivia, for example. US passport holders are required to obtain a visa and pay $160. Europeans? No visa, no fee. Other South American countries charge US, Canadian, Australian, and a smattering of other nationals "Reciprocity Fees," which run in the neighborhood of $140. Ouch. Also, Asian countries sometimes have different fees for Europeans than for US citizens. The advantage always goes to the Europeans, if there is one.

Logistics: It is completely legal to travel with two passports, but you need to know which one to present when. In general, you will be in better shape traveling on your European passport, so that is the passport you should present on arrival in a foreign country. If you checked into a country on your European passport, then you must check out with your European passport. Once you are in no-man's land, that time between checking out of one country and checking into the next, you can swap nationalities if it is in your best interest. The only time you'll likely gain an advantage by using your US passport, though, is on re-entry to the States.

Back-up

Once you receive your passport, take a photo of it or scan it. Email the electronic copy to yourself, or store it on a cloud storage service so you can retrieve it from anywhere. Also, make a paper copy and keep it in a location separate from your passport such as your main bag. If you lose your passport or it is stolen, it's helpful to have a copy when applying for a replacement. In addition to your passport, make copies of everything in your wallet. Copy the front and back of your credit cards, your driver's license, your insurance cards, etc. If your wallet is stolen, you will still have all of the information you need to cancel your credit cards or use your health insurance, and that will hopefully ease the pain of getting replacements.

Visas

Depending upon your nationality some countries require a visa. Visas may need to be obtained in advance, although they are frequently issued on arrival at your destination. Some visa applications also require proof of onward travel, and almost all require a fee. Check before you go and be prepared with the proper documents, payment method, and photos. A good resource for knowing if a visa is required is WorldTravelGuide.net. From the Country Guides menu, first select the continent and then the country you will be visiting. In the Before You Go section, there is a link for Passport and Visa. You can also check travel.state.gov. If you find that a visa is required, search for the application form online to be absolutely certain you have everything you need.

> *"We were attempting to get our Brazilian visas in the two days that we planned on being in Santiago, an infuriating process during which we got to know ... [a particular] bridge very well as we repeatedly trod from our hostel to the Brazilian consulate and to points in between. The really annoying part was that the people at the consulate didn't tell us until we had the proper-sized photos with the proper-colored background, copies of our credit cards, the addresses and phone numbers of our hotels in Brazil, evidence of payment for the visa at a bank in cash as well as copies of our bank statements for the last three months, that the process would take four working days. Ugh! That was the point at which we*

*aborted the mission in Santiago and planned on
completing the task in Buenos Aires."*

**Learning the Hard Way to Be Prepared for a Visa
Application**

Don't have a frustrating experience like ours. Be prepared
with the proper documents and form of payment. Know how
long the process will take. When applying for a visa you will
need the following items and useful information:

Color Photograph
Most applications will require one or two passport photos.
Before heading to parts of the world with countries requiring
visas, print extras so you are prepared. In our case, we are
never certain which countries we may visit, so it's good to
have a few photos handy. Double-check the size and
background color requirements for the specific visa for which
you are applying. As mentioned above, you can obtain the
passport photos at most drugstores and many other
retailers, or you can print them yourself.

Application Form
If the visa is to be issued on arrival, the form will be provided
at the point of entry and you will fill it out there. Countries
that require you to obtain your visa beforehand from a
consulate will expect the form to be filled out in advance.
Check to see if a photocopy of the application is also
required. Interestingly, it seems that the photocopy and
photo stores near the consulates are always a bit pricey.
Hmmm...

Address in the Country
The name and address of your first hotel or other lodging is
sufficient. If you don't have a reservation yet, look up a hotel
where you "might" stay. This always seemed like a silly thing
to ask for on an application since people tend to move
around when they are traveling.

Proof of Onward Travel
A round-trip airline ticket is the most common proof of onward travel. If you have arrived on a one-way ticket, though, it's a little bit tricky, especially if you plan to country-hop by bus, like in Southeast Asia. So, what do you do? Well, there are a couple of options. One is to book a refundable bus or plane ticket to somewhere out of the country within the period that the visa is valid, then cancel it. Another is to go online and fill out all of the steps to purchase a ticket, print the itinerary with your name on it, then don't actually buy it. You run some risk that the immigration officer will attempt to confirm your reservation, but that would take a lot of time and effort. We have used this trick once or twice, and our application was never scrutinized closely, but understand that there is some risk involved and you could potentially be denied entry into the country.

Proof of Funds
When applying for a visa prior to arrival, it's not uncommon to be asked to provide proof that you have enough money to afford traveling in the country and won't be seeking employment instead. Usually a recent bank statement is preferred. Look up the application form online and you'll find that a list of acceptable forms of proof of funds is usually provided.

Proof of Residency
A driver's license or a utility bill from your home country should suffice. Again, check the application form online and you'll find a list of acceptable proof of residency evidence. A note from your mother is unlikely to be on that list, though, so don't even bug her for one.

Fee
Be sure to have the fee in the proper form. It varies widely by country. A credit card is often acceptable, but sometimes you need cash and frequently that cash needs to be in the local currency. Occasionally, US dollars are accepted. Be aware, too, that sometimes you need to have the exact amount. Check before you go.

More on Visas

Visas are usually good for 30, 60, 90, or even 180 days. Be sure you know for how long your visa is valid and do not overstay. It is straightforward for most countries. Enter the country, receive a visa for so-many days, leave the country within that many days. Some countries have no restrictions on how soon you can return and receive a new visa, so you may be able to do a "visa-run" if you need more time. Simply, exit the country and then re-enter. Additionally, if you need more time in a country, especially in the event of an emergency, it is often possible to request an extension.

The Schengen

You know how I said that knowing how long you can stay in a country is straightforward for most countries? Well, there is the whole Schengen area in Europe to make things difficult.

What is the Schengen? Well, it's not the EU, though there are EU countries both in and out of the Schengen. There are also countries not in the EU that are in the Schengen. It's its own thing. At the time of writing, there are 26 member countries. Other countries are candidates and may be joining in the next couple of years. Bulgaria and Romania are probably next, and Croatia may be right behind them.

As a US citizen, you are permitted to stay in the Schengen for 90 days in a 180-day period without a visa. That is not a lot of time considering how many countries comprise the Schengen. What's more, it's a rolling 180 days, so keeping track of how many days in the last 180 you have been in the Schengen if you visit non-Schengen countries too can be a tricky task. I had to write a spreadsheet to keep track of that during our eight-month tour of Southern and Eastern Europe.

> *"Speaking of the border crossing... I made few friends there, and maybe that was why the driver was so crabby. When we arrived at the Greek/Bulgarian border, the Greek official came to the van and collected our passports to check us out of the country (and Schengen region in my case). Unfortunately, their system was down. It's cool. No problem. Oh wait, is that a US passport? Now we have a*

problem. The minivan driver was instructed to park off to the side. He looked at me the way a six-year-old scowls at a piece of broccoli. Everyone was handed back their passports, except for me (Pat travels on his French passport). After about 30 minutes of officials making phone calls and cross stares from most of my van mates, we were on our way."

How to Make Few Friends and Piss Off People

The cool thing is there is free movement between all of the Schengen countries. For instance, I almost didn't notice when we crossed from Spain into France (the Pyrenees tipped me off). The bummer is, you only get two passport stamps! You receive an entry stamp from the first Schengen country you visit and an exit stamp from the last. The only way to collect more stamps is to travel out of the Schengen and back in through another country.

If you are planning a multiple-month trip to Europe and are subject to the 90 days in 180 days restriction, be sure to know which of your destinations are in the Schengen and which are not. Here is a helpful map: www.schengenvisainfo.com/schengen-visa-countries-list/ .

Yellow Fever Certificate

One souvenir no one wants is a nasty disease. Make sure you are current with your routine vaccines (measles-mumps-rubella, diphtheria-tetanus-pertussis, chickenpox, polio), and check to see if any other vaccines are recommended for where you are going. The CDC gives a list of recommendations by country. In general, if you are going to an equatorial region, additional vaccines will likely be recommended, as well as malaria medicine.

What do vaccinations have to do with Travel Documents? Well, you may be required to show your yellow fever vaccination certificate in order to be granted entry to the country. If you plan to visit a country where there's a risk of yellow fever transmission, be sure to carry your certificate. In all of our travels, we were only asked to produce ours once, and that was in Ecuador when we arrived by sailboat. Here is a list of countries and their yellow fever certificate requirements: www.who.int/ith/ITH_country_list.pdf , and here is a map of areas where yellow fever is more prevalent: www.cdc.gov/yellowfever/maps/.

Tickets and Reservations

Nowadays most airline, bus, attraction, and lodging reservations and purchases are made online. Although you can usually access the reservation or ticket via an app, it's a good idea to print it, if at all possible. A paper copy means that you're not out of luck if your phone goes dead. Keep in mind, too, that some of the airlines require a paper copy of your boarding pass.

For even greater peace of mind, also save the reservation or ticket as a pdf, and store it on a cloud-based storage service. Google Drive is free and has enough storage for a large number of pdfs. Make sure Google Drive, or whichever cloud storage service you use, is synced with your smartphone and any other device you may use for accessing the document. Also, be sure to enable the files for viewing offline.

Insurance

"So, was I [Pat] to be the recipient of the heavenly relaxation that I so desperately needed, or a slice of Las Vegas with its neon and glitter and party animals? The short answer is that I got a bit of both and then some. The 'then some' came in the form of a low-grade infection, probably food poisoning, that resulted in a trip to the ship's ER and a 24-hour in-cabin quarantine. Repositioning cruises don't make many landfalls — this one made only two stops — and I missed the first one in Malaga, Spain, due to the quarantine. Fortunately, the plague lasted only two days, and I was released from prison on my own recognizance. Not a good start to our Atlantic crossing, eh?"

Pat Racking up a Serious Medical Bill on a Cruise Ship

DO NOT travel without insurance! I know, you are young and invincible, or you have Medicare or a plan through the US healthcare exchange, or you don't want to waste money on something you won't use. I hear you, but broken bones happen, luggage gets stolen, emergency evacuations can be necessary. Without insurance and the proper coverage, you'll quickly blow a hole clean through your travel kitty if you succumb to a serious mishap.

Depending on where you plan to travel, how long you plan to travel, how old you are, what insurance you already have, and what coverage you want, the type of insurance you need will vary. Of course, it's complicated, as it seems all insurance is, but I'll make sense of it in a moment. I won't dwell on this subject for too long, either, because it is terribly boring, and there is no one-size-fits-all policy. You will need to do some research on your own, but I will give you the resources to do it. Besides, I have only one story, but having only one story, in this case, is a good thing.

International Travel Insurance

In nearly all circumstances, international travel insurance is what you need, and the good news is that there are plans with enough coverage for the average traveler at low rates. If you are traveling internationally for a few months, it doesn't make sense for you to cancel your regular health insurance policy. A travel insurance policy can cover you for accidents and sudden illnesses and can even pay for your transfer back to home in the event of a death in your family.

Travel insurance generally also covers trip cancellations (for covered reasons, so check the details of the plan you are considering), trip interruptions (ditto), and stolen/lost baggage. Pat and I have found plans that fit our needs, at reasonable prices, at insuremytrip.com.

International Health Insurance

International health insurance and international travel insurance are two entirely different things. International health insurance is much more comprehensive and correspondingly more expensive. It's meant for expats or people traveling abroad for a year or more. With international health insurance, routine wellness exams, prescription medicines, and office visits are covered, whereas international travel insurance is really just for emergencies and is meant to patch you up and send you home.

I have purchased international health insurance often due to our penchant for being in exotic places for years at a time, but beware of US health insurance rules. Over the past two years, I carried international health insurance with a US rider (an add-on to my international policy since I had terminated my regular US insurance) because we were goofing around in Southeast Asia and Europe for most of that time. The Affordable Care Act health insurance mandate made things a little sketchy, though, because we came back for a visit to the US during the two years. I had to watch how many days I stayed in the States or else be subject to a hefty fine for not having ACA-approved insurance, even though I actually did have insurance. The rules change quickly, and as of now, the individual mandate has been repealed, but it is still in place for 2018. Be sure you know how dropping your US plan can affect you.

Luckily, we found an excellent trustworthy agent and have recommended him to friends. Neither Pat nor I has ever made a claim, but one of our friends has, and he was very happy with the customer support and claim process. Our agent's name is Alonso Cornejo at ASA (480)-753-1333 and he has been our agent since 2005. He and his staff are international travel insurance experts, and they will guide you to the plan that best fits your needs. Be sure to tell them that Pat and Carrie Kinnison sent you!

Accidental Death and Dismemberment

When you buy the least expensive travel insurance plan that you can find, it will likely not have accidental death and dismemberment coverage. If you already have a life insurance policy or a disability policy, confirm that it covers you internationally. In case you want D&D coverage while on your trip and don't otherwise have coverage, you can find inexpensive policies at insuremytrip.com. D&D policies pay a lump-sum in the event of death or dismemberment. They have no deductible, but they may cost you an arm or a leg to collect on.

Medicare/Medigap

Medicare does not cover medical expenses outside of the US, except in certain extenuating circumstances such as being trampled by a moose while making your way from

Alaska to the lower 48 by the most direct route. In that case, you're covered if your injuries are life-threatening and the nearest hospital is Canadian. That's about it, so don't count on basic Medicare.

Medigap, however, usually does offer some coverage. It is also known as Medicare part G, C, D, E, F, H, I, J, M, or N. You might think that I'm trying to be funny, but there really are that many Medicare parts for Medigap. Maybe they should call it MediScare instead. Anyway, if you have a Medigap policy, you will likely have international emergency medical coverage for the first 60 days of your trip. If you are traveling for only two months, it may be enough coverage for you. Obviously, it won't cover lost bags or trip cancellations, but you can choose to buy a travel insurance policy to fill those holes. Check your specific Medigap policy since coverage varies.

Medigap saved Pat quite a few Benjamins on the cruise mentioned in the blog snippet at the start of this chapter. The bill for his IV fluids, antibiotics, and doctor's exam came to $1,800! We were both extremely happy that his plan picked up 80% of that (after he had met his deductible).

Credit Card Travel Insurance

Pay attention to what credit card you use to buy large, non-refundable, travel-related expenses: flights, cruises, tours, etc. Some credit cards offer travel insurance (cancellations, interruptions, etc.) on purchases made with the card. Other credit cards, ones with an annual fee, offer full-blown travel insurance, providing coverage that includes medical emergencies and evacuations. If none of your cards offer any travel insurance (the importance of having a credit card with rental car insurance is covered in the Transportation chapter), do a search for "best travel insurance credit card." Each year, independent reviewers such as TripSavvy, Forbes, and WalletHub make lists of the best travel credit cards, comparing their costs and benefits. Make sure there are no foreign transaction fees either.

Insurance Lingo

The insurance industry has a vernacular of its own. If you are dealing with an agent or just reading through your coverage literature, you are going to run into some terms that you may not know. It is important to understand at least the following terms so that you are not surprised when making a claim.

- Deductible — This is the amount you will need to pay out of pocket before the insurance company pays any expenses. You need to balance this with the policy's premium. If you select a plan with a low deductible, the premium will be higher than the premium of a high-deductible plan. Think of it like buying a large umbrella or a small umbrella. The large umbrella will cost more, but if it rains, you won't get as wet.
- Premium — This is the amount that you pay for the insurance policy. The deductible you select influences the amount of the premium. The higher the deductible, the lower the premium.
- Copayment/Coinsurance — Both of these terms describe how much a covered expense will cost during the time after you have met your deductible but before you have reached your out-of-pocket maximum. Copayment is a dollar amount, whereas coinsurance is a percentage. So, if a covered office visit is $100 and your copayment is $15, you pay $15 for the office visit. On the other hand, if your coinsurance is 20%, you will pay $20 for the same office visit.
- Max Out-of-Pocket — After you have spent the max out-of-pocket amount between the deductible and copayments/coinsurance, your plan will pay 100% of subsequently covered expenses. Your accumulated expenses will also reset to zero each plan year.
- Lifetime Maximum Limit — This is the maximum amount of money that the insurance company will pay to you during your lifetime. Plans may offer different lifetime maximum limits. The higher the limit, the higher your premium.

- Medical Underwriting — The insurance company may require a medical exam and/or a medical history before issuing you a policy. Certain pre-existing conditions may prevent you from getting a policy, or exclusions may apply.

Discuss all of this with your insurance agent so that you are absolutely certain that what you are getting is what you want.

Technology

*"'Dear Mom and Dad, send money and socks.' Did you
ever wonder how we answered emails while on the road?
No? Maybe a few of you? Well, some of the hostels
provided one or two computers where we could check our
email for free. They were usually turn-of-the-century
machines with no USB ports, no CD-burner, and
processing power equivalent to a hamster on a wheel.
But, hey, we were just happy to read all of your emails."*

**Back in the Day when Internet Cafés Were Pretty
Cool - Tierra del Fuego, Circa 2008**

Technology has come a long way in the blink of an eye. Just
ten years ago, smartphones weren't a thing and Wi-Fi was
far from ubiquitous. Traveling with a laptop back then was
uncommon because they were too darn big and heavy.
Email was checked at most once a day, usually from an
internet café or a shared computer at a hostel.

Smartphones, tablets, ultra-light laptops, and widely
available Wi-Fi have completely changed how people travel.
Most of the change is good, but there certainly are pitfalls
too. Being too connected can remove you from the here and
now. In all likelihood, you are not going to visit the same city
or town twice. A few places maybe, but most you won't.
Don't fall into the social media vortex and miss the

uniqueness of life going on around you. Set rules, if necessary.

Things change quickly on the technology front, but here is what we are traveling with right now:

<u>Chromebook</u>

The Chromebook is the latest addition to my electronic gear. Until early 2017, I had been writing my blog posts on a smartphone. Trust me, that is an excruciatingly slow process. A Bluetooth keyboard for the phone was an option, but even with that I'd be squinting uncomfortably at a tiny screen. That's when I discovered Chromebooks.

Before getting into the pluses and minuses of a Chromebook, let's briefly discuss "the Cloud" because it is central to what makes Chromebooks powerful yet affordable. The Cloud isn't as nebulous as it sounds. It is simply a term used for the computers and storage devices connected to the internet that run programs for you or store your files. The Cloud makes it possible to run complicated programs and store massive amounts of data (think photos and videos) using a computer with modest processing power and limited storage. For instance, Google Drive is a form of cloud-based storage where you can save files and then retrieve them from anywhere as long as you have an internet connection. It looks and acts just like an internal hard drive, but it isn't physically in your computer. Similarly, Google Docs is a good example of a program being run "in the Cloud." I can type away on a document in Docs on my Chromebook and later, if I think of something to add, I can open my document on my smartphone, or even a public computer, and work on it from there. There is no software to install. The document is synced and saved automatically. (I will discuss syncing, short for synchronizing, shortly.)

Though the Chromebook is generally meant to be used while online via Wi-Fi, it is possible to store files in its internal memory and use programs while offline. Let's say you're writing the Great American Novel using Google Docs. If you want to work on your novel while offline, there are two things you need to do. First, since you will not have access to the cloud computer that runs the Docs software, you need to install the Google Docs app on your Chromebook. To do so, go to the app store, search for Google Docs, and then click "+Add to Chrome." The second thing you need to do is turn the sync feature on. You can do this by opening Google Drive and clicking on the gear icon in the upper right. Then select "Settings." Make sure the check-box for "offline" is checked. Now, you can work on your novel anywhere, and when your Chromebook connects to the internet again, the edits you made while sitting in a tent somewhere in the middle of the Amazon rainforest will sync with the files stored in the Cloud.

In a vast departure from early-2000's laptops, the Chromebook weighs only about 2lbs, isn't bulky, and costs around $200. The battery life is outstanding, and the keyboard is comfortable. The particular Chromebook I purchased is made by Asus, and I love it. It's sturdy, too. In fact, a spider just leaped from nowhere onto my keyboard while I was writing (seriously, I'm not making this up), and I jettisoned the Chromebook halfway across the room. The Chromebook survived the crash-landing without a ding, but my coffee spilled all over the floor leaving me desperately short on caffeine. I hate spiders.

Ok, that's enough about spiders, so back to the Chromebook. My needs are fairly uncomplicated. I read and write emails, post on Facebook and Twitter, do a little photo manipulation, listen to music, stream video from YouTube or Amazon Prime, book rooms and flights, and read guidebooks. I use Google Maps... a lot. And, of course, I write blog posts and am currently writing chapters for this book with Google Docs. The Chromebook is perfectly suited for these needs. It has made my on-the-road writing much less of a task, and it is easy to carry.

A cool feature of the Chromebook is that it has an HDMI output so that the screen can be shared on newer televisions. It is perfect for presenting slideshows or videos to large, captive audiences. (Pro Tip: Provide ample wine if you are showing travel photos.) The other day, I wanted to share a travel show that I'd seen on Amazon Prime, so I simply connected the Chromebook to the Wi-Fi, connected the HDMI cable between the Chromebook and the television, switched the television input to the proper HDMI port, signed into my Amazon Prime account, and streamed the show on the big screen. Tah dah! Everyone could enjoy the show without having to huddle around a tiny laptop.

What a Chromebook cannot do: It has no optical drive, so it can't play DVDs or CDs. Programs such as Photoshop, CAD (Computer-Aided Design), or stock trading platforms (thinkorswim, StreetSmart Edge, etc.) can't be installed. The operating system is Chrome, not Windows or iOS, so you are limited to Chrome extensions, Chrome apps, Android apps, and web-based apps. The good news is that there are many high-quality Chrome apps, Chrome extensions, and Android apps. They can be found through the Chrome Web Store. A shortcut comes pre-installed on Chromebooks.

Chromebook apps and extensions that I am finding particularly useful include the following:

Antivirus
You don't need it! It is built in and is automatically kept up-to-date.

TunnelBear VPN
If you plan to use public Wi-Fi hotspots, it is wise to keep hackers at bay by running a VPN (Virtual Private Network). Hackers can potentially see your data if you are not using a VPN, and that's really not a good thing if you are plugging in your credit card number to buy tickets or something else online. Tunnelbear offers a Chrome extension, and with one subscription you can protect all of your devices, including ones running iOS, macOS, Windows, Android, or Chrome. Tunnelbear is easy to use and can be running on five devices simultaneously. The subscription is free for up to 500MB in a month (that's not much data), or you can upgrade to unlimited data for $7.99/month or $49.99/year. So, if you are going away for six months or more, you might as well pay for the year.

Kindle Cloud Reader
As the name implies, this app is for reading your Kindle books on the Cloud. The Cloud Reader allows you to download your books to the hard drive for offline access. Reading guidebooks on the Chromebook is much easier than on the smartphone, but it is convenient to have that option too.

Snapseed
This is a photo-editing app that can be used offline. The free version can do all of the usual things: crop, adjust lighting and color, apply filters, add text, draw shapes, and much more. The free version is powerful enough for what I do and is intuitive to use.

Google Docs
Docs is the Chrome version of Microsoft Word and is nearly a doppelgänger of Word. You can format text, add tables, insert photos, create lists, and basically do all the things you typically need to do when writing a document. Since the documents are stored in the Cloud, you can also collaborate on them with other people. In addition, you can allow other people to edit, read-only, or make comments.

As mentioned above, you also need to make sure that the "offline" setting in Google Drive is checked in order to sync the documents you saved for offline editing with your cloud documents. There will be more on the Google suite of apps and how to sign up for a Google account later.

Google Hangouts Dialer
Well, you have to stay in touch with people back home, right? Your parents would go nuts if you didn't phone them every so often to let them know that you are okay, after all. The Google Hangouts Dialer app can dial phones in the US and Canada for free using VoIP (Voice over Internet Protocol). For phones outside of the US and Canada, Hangouts offers low rates that vary depending on the country you are calling. If you plan to call people in countries that are not free, add credit through the app with a credit card and dial away. You will be able to make calls until your account runs dry, but keep it topped up or you might get cut

off in mid... Of course, if you are calling or video-calling another Google Hangouts user anywhere in the world, it's free.

In order to make phone calls, you need to install both the Hangouts app and the Hangouts Dialer app. After you have installed both apps, launch either Hangouts or Hangouts Dialer when you want to initiate a phone call. Click on the icon that looks like an old Ma Bell handset (do millennials even know what that is?), and then type in the phone number you wish to call.

Be aware, you can't use Google Hangouts to make calls from the following countries: Argentina, China, Cuba, Egypt, Ghana, India (Users in India can make calls to all countries except to locations within India.), Iran, Jordan, Kenya, Mexico, Morocco, Myanmar, Nigeria, North Korea, Peru, Russian Federation, Saudi Arabia, Senegal, South Korea, Sudan, Syria, Thailand, United Arab Emirates, Vietnam. The list is subject to change. Check Google Support for the latest information.

Skype
Skype is our favorite VoIP phone-calling app. It is the original, and we have been using it since shortly after its release. The call quality is excellent, and it's installed on all of our devices - the Chromebook, the Surface, and the smartphone.

Furthermore, Skype-to-Skype calls are free. The rate to call a US or Canadian landline or mobile from anywhere in the world is 2.3 cents per minute. Skype also offers subscriptions with unlimited calling throughout the world for $13.99/month or to only North America for $6.99/month. Some destinations, like the UK, have complicated rate plans based on whether you are calling a landline or a mobile phone and who the provider is.

Skype also offers a service where you can have an incoming phone number, called a Skype Number. This is a great way to let friends and family back home call you at their local rates. For example, I can select a Tucson phone number. My friends and family then call it like any other Tucson phone number and are charged their normal local-calling rates. The service is offered in 3-month or 12-month subscriptions. For a US number, the 3-month subscription is $18.53 and the 12-month subscription is $52.26.

Facebook Messenger
You can also make voice and video calls for free to anyone who has Facebook Messenger installed. Just click on the Messenger icon (bubble with a lightning bolt in it), select the person you want to call, then click the Ma Bell handset icon for voice-calling or the movie camera icon for video-calling.

Amazon Cloud Drive
I once read that if you don't have your photos in at least two places, you don't have your photos. We subscribe to Amazon Prime, and one of its benefits is unlimited photo storage. This app gives us quick access to our Amazon Cloud Drive so that we can easily upload, download, or view our photos and files.

Typically, I snap photos constantly with my phone while roaming around wherever we are. When I return to my room, I cull the day's photos on the phone and then send the keepers to a descriptively named folder on my Amazon Cloud Drive. The naming convention I use for folders is yyyy_mm_dd_location (e.g. 2018_05_14_LasVegasNevadaUSA). I'm sure you can see how this naming convention makes it easy to sort by date or search by location.

When I want to use a photo in a blog post or on Facebook, I download the photo to the Chromebook from my Amazon Cloud Drive, manipulate it a little bit with Snapseed, and then upload it to the blog post or Facebook. Pat also stores his photos on our shared Amazon Cloud Drive, so if I want to use his photos, they are there too.

Google Keep
This is a handy app, great for notes and making lists. It can also save links to web pages you may want to access at a later date, and it syncs across all of your devices, so you can

write your shopping list on your laptop and then access it from your smartphone.

The reminder feature is innovative, too. As usual, you can set a date and time to be reminded, or you can set a location, like a grocery store. When you walk into the grocery store, you can have your shopping list pop up on your phone. Just be sure Keep is installed on your phone, too.

Google Maps

This is a web app. Obviously, it is great for looking at maps, but you can mark places that you plan to visit, find phone numbers, check bus or train schedules, and obtain walking, driving, or public transport directions. You can also see reviews of restaurants, hotels, monuments, attractions, and parks. The only drawback is that you cannot save a map for offline use on the Chromebook. Fortunately, the smartphone picks up the slack here.

Heidi's Infinite Sudoku

All work and no play...

Smartphone

I am sure you've noticed by now all of the Google references, so it should come as no surprise that we carry a smartphone with the Android operating system. Our current phone is a Samsung Galaxy S5. I struggle to call it a smartphone because we probably use it for making phone calls least of all. SmartCamera or SmartGPS more accurately describes its function.

> *"The address we were given for our Airbnb "pod" was a latitude and longitude. The Google navigation app on the smartphone took us to the coordinates, but we didn't see a pod. The property was a bit run-down, and a dog in the yard looked at us menacingly. Pat suggested that I get out to see if anyone was in the house. See how he is? Just because I booked the Airbnb meant he could throw me to the hounds.*

I got out of the Irish Porsche, which was honestly much nicer than any of the vehicles in the driveway, and I was barked at a few times before the old dog lost interest. By the time I got to the door, a man had come outside. I asked about the pod, mentioned Airbnb, and got the dreaded 'I have absolutely no idea what you are talking about' look and a thick, indecipherable response saying as much. Great. Muff isn't technically in Northern Ireland, but thankfully the cell service still worked. I called the number given on Airbnb for the listing. Voicemail. I left a message."

Navigating, Using the Airbnb App, and Making a Phone Call While Lost in Ireland

If I had to recommend one piece of technology for the average traveler to take along, it would be a smartphone. Hands down. It's a camera. It's a library. It's a web-surfer. It's a navigator. It's a weatherman. It's even a phone. It's the Swiss army knife that any good scout should have in his or her kit.

Which Smartphone?

Here is the part where you figure that I'm going to say that you must carry an Android phone since I mention Google non-stop. Not so. I totally understand brand loyalty and that Apple products have a huge following. The important thing to find out is whether your phone/operating system supports the apps that you want to run. Can it be, or is it, unlocked? (I'll explain what "unlocked" is in a moment.) Does it support GSM (Global System for Mobile communication) technology? GSM is used worldwide, but if you bought a phone in the States, it might not support GSM. Certain US carriers, Verizon being one, use a different technology though the phones they sell may accommodate both technologies.

The two largest mobile phone operating systems are iOS (Apple) and Android (Google). Over 95% of all smartphones run on one of those two operating systems. Not surprisingly, developers create apps that run on iOS and/or Android before any other OS. It follows then that the largest selection of apps can be found for Apple and Android phones. Sure, that makes sense, but what does "unlocked" mean? An unlocked phone is simply one that is capable of being used with any service provider. If you are not sure if your phone is unlocked, take it to your provider's store and ask them.

Phone Cameras

Will this be your primary camera? If so, read the reviews online and make sure the optics and flash are good. Are you a selfie-taking-type? Please tell me you aren't. Lie if you have to, but if you are, check the reviews on the self-facing camera because self-facing cameras often take photos of inferior quality. Make sure you can put at least a 64 gigabyte SD (Secure Digital) card into your phone, if not a 128 gigabyte card. By having all of that memory, you can shoot photos and videos for a long long time before running out of space. The SD card also serves as one of the two locations for your photos. Remember, if you don't have your photos in at least two places, you don't have your photos. Be sure to back up regularly to a cloud service and/or an external device. It is our routine to back up nightly to our Amazon Drive on the Cloud.

Memory

Your smartphone has two types of memory, internal and removable. The internal memory in my ancient Samsung Galaxy S5 is only 16 gigabytes and can't be upgraded. Newer phones have more internal memory, which is a good thing because it is easy to run into memory problems when you have only 16 gigabytes, even when no superfluous apps are installed. When you install an app on your smartphone, it is put into the internal memory. Not only that, but the app saves bits of data as it is used. That's called caching, and cached data goes into the internal memory too.

The removable memory in your smartphone is also known as an SD card. Instead of leaving an app installed in the internal memory, many apps can be moved to the SD card. If you are running into memory issues, try moving apps to the SD card, and be sure to install the largest SD card as possible, especially if you take a lot of photos, videos, or are on a multi-month trip. In addition to the SD card being one location for storing your photos and videos, you can store music, movies, and other files there too. The Galaxy S5 can handle up to a 128 gigabyte SD card. Check the specs for your particular smartphone.

WIreless Data / Calling / Texting
International data and calling plans through US cell service providers are quite expensive. A much more budget-friendly option is to buy a prepaid plan in the country you are visiting. This is why it is important to have an unlocked phone with GSM capability. In the US, some carriers use CDMA (Code-Division Multiple Access) technology, but most of the rest of the world uses GSM. Your phone may support both technologies or only one. If you have an unlocked phone that works on GSM, though, you can enjoy inexpensive cell phone service virtually anywhere in the world.

So, what is the process? Contact your host, or do a search online to find the service providers in the country you are visiting. Make sure the voice and data coverage maps include where you plan to visit. Read reviews. Once you've selected a provider, head to one of their stores and ask for a prepaid voice/data plan. They always have a menu of plans. Choose the one that is right for your needs. Some plans have more gigabytes of data. Others have more minutes of voice calling, and some offer unlimited texting within the country. The next thing that happens is that the tech replaces your SIM (Subscriber Identity Module) card with a new one. It's a painless procedure to have a SIM card installed. Remove the case on your phone, if you have one, and the tech will do the rest. After a couple of these experiences, you'll be disassembling your phone for the tech. A note of caution, if you plan to use the SIM card that was removed again, be sure to put it in a safe place! Some phones have dual SIM card slots which is nice since you can leave your "home" card installed and not worry about losing it.

A one-month 1- to 2-gigabyte data plan in Europe that includes some amount of calling and texting within the country can run as little as $10. Usually, SIM cards are free, but if not, they run around $10. Important tip: You will need to show your passport in order to buy service. Once, in Verona, Italy, we walked three miles to buy a plan for the phone and forgot our passports. It turned into a 12-mile day. Good thing beers were cheap and our route had plenty of watering holes.

Do you really need a wireless plan? Well, if you are renting a car, I'd strongly suggest it for navigation. It's also worth having so you can call or text your host if you are running late. Is it a must-have? No. Is it really nice to have? Yes. For roughly $10/month, it's hard to pass up. Also, in Europe, roaming has been free since the summer of 2017. What that means is that when you enter a different country, you no longer need to sign up with a new provider. For instance, we signed up with a provider and bought a plan in Romania just before the free roaming went into effect. Instead of signing up with a new provider in each new European country we visited after that, we kept recharging our Romanian plan at 6€ for three weeks (I have no idea why it was three weeks) and used it all through Hungary, Croatia, Italy, France, and Spain. The only drawback was that the texts from the Romanian provider were in Romanian and so were the recharging instructions!

One last note, TEST your wireless data connection BEFORE you leave the store. Usually the tech sets up your plan through a Wi-Fi connection in the store. They always do a test voice call and usually a test text, but they almost never remember to disconnect from the store's Wi-Fi to test the data connection. Be sure to confirm that your phone is disconnected from the Wi-Fi, and try accessing a website, VinoHiking.com, for instance. If it doesn't work, it may be because some networks need to configure an APN (Access Point Name) in order for the data connection to work. I learned about this the hard way in Italy when the data connection was tested over Wi-Fi and not through the carrier's service. We walked a long way back to the apartment and then discovered that the data didn't work. Fortunately, our host knew exactly what to do. He was an IT guy!

We went all out and took a taxi from Struga, Macedonia to Berat, Albania. The deal went down in a dusty parking lot where we were supposed to catch the first of three buses for a 7+ hour journey to Berat. The taxi driver didn't speak much English, but he understood "how much?" and "how long?" The price-to-comfort ratio was reasonable and the taxi fare fit in our budget. Woohoo! First class for us!

Three hours later, we pulled into Berat. I showed the driver the name of our guesthouse and pointed at a location on Google Maps. He seemed unimpressed with the technology in the palm of my hand. "No worries, no problem," he said, then "Telephone?" I pulled up the telephone number and indicated that I didn't have voice service on my phone, only data. He apparently didn't have Albanian voice service on his flip-phone either since he was Macedonian. "No problem, no worries," he said as he smiled. He pulled up to a young man near the central park, asked him a very brief question, then snatched the young man's phone. The young man smiled and stood there patiently. Our driver called the guesthouse, returned the phone to the young man and off we went. No worries, no problems! The guesthouse was very near.

Or... Just Use Any Stranger's Phone.

Smartphone Apps

If you are traveling with only a smartphone, you'll have a large number of apps, but if you are traveling with a second internet-connected device, such as a laptop, you can offload some of the work to it, like finding flights and editing photos. Many of the apps below are the mobile version of ones I mentioned above for the Chromebook. Apps that I find useful and recommend are the following:

Google Maps
Surprise! I bet you're flabbergasted that Google Maps is one of my recommendations. Well, for starters, even without a data connection you can use Google Maps to find your way around. While you have Wi-Fi or a data connection, and you search an area on Google Maps, the app does a certain amount of caching (storing of data) so that when you don't

have a data connection, you can still use the map. If you want to be absolutely certain that you have access to a map offline, save it to your "offline areas." Maps can consume quite a bit of memory, so purge them when you move on, and check the settings to make sure that you're storing the maps on the SD card rather than on the internal memory. If you rely on the automatic caching that the app does, DO NOT clear your device's cached data!

> *"We spent most of the early morning train ride in the dining car administering caffeine to ourselves and saying goodbye to my brother. I started getting nervous about the randomness of my selection for our overnight pit stop when station after station appeared abandoned with no signs of life. I sure hope Pat isn't noticing this. I wanted to check our progress on Google Maps, but to make matters more agitating, I had cleared the cache on the phone the night before. Google Maps was rendered useless without a Wi-Fi connection. Now I couldn't even tell at which weather-worn, dusty, boarded-up station to get off the train.*
>
> *The conductor came by and told us our station was next. The station we passed didn't look very promising and was possibly abandoned. 'Are you sure you know where we're going?' asked Pat. Uh-oh, he noticed. What have I gotten us into this time?"*

En Route to Palmela, Portugal

Another reason why Google Maps tops my list is that you can mark on it locations that you like or want to visit. When you search for, say a restaurant, you not only see it on the map, but the phone number is given too (click to call). A link to the website, reviews, photos, and hours of operation are also provided. It's one-stop shopping with Google Maps.

Google Maps Navigation
Yes, this is the same Google Maps app as above, but this function deserves special mention because it is invaluable when renting a car. When we plan on renting a car, we purchase a data plan for the smartphone. It is possible to

navigate with maps saved to "offline areas," but having an actual data connection gives us peace of mind, and we can search for restaurants and gas stations while on the road too. The Google B*tch, the name that we affectionately call the voice that gives the turn-by-turn directions, has guided us over thousands of miles of mostly roads. I say "mostly" because a few were roads in only the loosest sense. One that comes to mind was in Wales. She guided us over highways to two-lane roads, then eventually to a single-track lane. For many miles, our side mirrors brushed grass taller than the car, and we kept our fingers crossed that no one was speeding toward us. She gets in moods sometimes, but we have always made it to our destination in the end.

Now that the mode of transportation is set, one must figure out where to go and in what order. We rely heavily on our traveling companion, the grand lady of navigation, the ever-present eye in the sky, our dear friend, The Google B*tch. She sometimes finds roads so narrow that we have to fold in the mirrors to prevent them from being ripped off the car. There are also times that I swear she is leading us to the edge of the world, to be swallowed up by demons in the abyss. At other times, I think that she just wants to toy with us (she has a great, albeit sick, sense of humor) to see how trusting we are of her skills, because when things get dicey, she always finds an alternate route. Trust is a must, and as long as you keep her properly juiced and supply her with a healthy serving of data, she will steer you to some heavenly destinations.

Trusting the Google B*tch to Get Us Where We're Going

You can never have too many Google B*tch stories...

The directions given to us by our Airbnb host were to pull into town, and her place would be the one across the street from the bakery, number seven. That sounded easy.

We arrived in Fronsac and drove down the main street. It was a tiny town. We didn't see the bakery, so we drove

back the way we came and looked again. No bakery. Pat
asked a man for directions to the bakery and then drove
to it. Strangely, it wasn't on the main road and there was
no number seven nearby. Nous sommes perdus again.

I double-checked the instructions and noticed it was not
Fronsac but Saint Michel de Fronsac where we were
supposed to be. Ah! A nice man outside the Fronsac
government offices gave us directions to Saint Michel de
Fronsac and told us we couldn't possibly miss the bakery.
We did. It's almost like we aren't even trying sometimes.

**Thinking We Probably Should Have Plugged the
Directions into Google Maps**

Maps.me and Citymapper

Although, Google Maps will be sufficient 99% of the time, there are a couple of other map apps that offer other features. Maps.me often has better coverage of hiking trails than Google Maps, so if you like to hike, it's worth checking out. Citymapper, though it only works in large cities, is great in that it not only gives you public transportation directions, but based on your final destination, it will actually tell you which subway exit to use. Don't you just hate it when you surface from the depths of the subway station blinking in the harsh daylight and discover that you're on the wrong side of a major boulevard?

TunnelBear

This was mentioned above, but again, if you plan to access email, Facebook, your bank account, or anything from your smartphone that you would rather not have hacked while using a Wi-Fi hotspot, you should use a VPN.

Booking.com

I'll get into more detail in the Accommodations chapter, but Booking.com is my go-to hotel/motel/guesthouse booking app. The mobile version is slick and makes finding a room a simple task.

Airbnb

Also mentioned in detail in the Accommodations chapter is the Airbnb app. It's a well-written app and easy to use, even from the phone.

Amazon Kindle

If you have a Kindle library or have subscribed to KindleUnlimited, you need this app in order to read your books on your smartphone. I am still amazed that I can carry around ten different guidebooks and the complete works of Mark Twain all at the same time without herniating anything.

Before you set out, make sure you have downloaded to your phone the books you want to read while you are offline. This is done simply by clicking on the Library icon and then selecting "All." Your purchased titles will then be displayed. Find the book that you want to have on your phone, and click on it to initiate the download process. You can confirm that the book is available offline by clicking on "Downloaded."

If you have a Kindle or use the Kindle reader on a laptop, your reading progress will be in sync across all of your devices. Bookmarks, highlights, and notes will also sync.

Amazon Drive

This app gives you quick access to your Amazon Drive and makes uploading photos from your smartphone a breeze. If you subscribe to Amazon Prime, you receive unlimited photo storage. The app is easy to use. Launch it, select the folder you want to upload your photos to, or create a new one, then click "Upload" and select the photos you want to put up in the Cloud. Once they are in the Cloud, you can access them from your laptop to process or use in a post.

Google Drive

Google has a cloud-based storage service too, one which offers 15 gigabytes of free storage. I use some of the free space for storing reservations, tickets, backups of our passports, etc. Google Docs, Sheets, and Slides are also stored there. It is convenient and can be accessed from anywhere with an internet connection. Documents can be made available offline too.

In a typical day, you might make a reservation for a room and buy a bus ticket online. Generally, you'll receive a confirmation or e-tickets in an email. Save the ticket or the confirmation as a .pdf file to your Google Drive. While you are looking at your Google Drive, check for files that you have previously marked for offline availability and deselect them if they are no longer needed. No sense using memory for things you don't need.

Dual Clock Widget
Is it too late or too early to call home? A dual clock widget stuck on your home screen will ensure that you don't ring anyone who is in a deep sleep. Set one clock to local time and the other to home time.

> *"The phone woke me up at about 4:30 in the morning with the Facebook notification sound. Who on earth would be messaging us? The parents didn't know how to use it. My brother and friends rarely used it, and never for emergencies. Everyone we knew in Europe was equally as dead asleep as we were.*
>
> *I rolled over and tried to go back to sleep. It was already light outside, not surprising. It was, after all, the summer solstice and we were at 52 degrees north in Pembrokeshire, Wales, in a small town called Newport.*
>
> *4:30am? Wasn't there something I wanted to do very early this morning? Whoa… Wait a minute… click, click, whir… the brain started to come back online. Holy crap! The Cavs must have won the championship!"*

> **Receiving Very Good News, But Very Early in the Morning**

Weather Underground Widget
Having the weather forecast at your fingertips is useful for knowing how warmly to dress and whether you should take an umbrella with you. Weather Underground has a compact and informative widget which is great on your home screen

as it shows the temperature at your current location and provides a three-day forecast in graph form. If you need more detail or the 10-day forecast, just click on the widget and you'll get the full scoop. It is most useful for picking the best day for your next VinoHike!

GasBuddy
When you're traveling by car in the US, GasBuddy is a must-have app. Is the tank running low? Launch GasBuddy and click the "Find Gas Near You" button. A list of stations sorted by distance and price for regular gas will be shown. You can also view the prices on a map, which I personally find easier. Keep an eye out for a little green icon next to the price, though. The price displayed is for cash, and it's lower than the price for credit/debit by five to ten cents per gallon.

Click on a station to see its hours of operation, rating (seriously, people write reviews for gas stations), and its prices (cash and credit/debit) for all grades of gas and diesel (if they have it). Once you have filled up, take a moment to confirm or report a change in the prices. That's how GasBuddy works. Motorists like you keep the prices updated so that others can find the least expensive gas too. Oh, and write a review... "The beef jerky was out of this world!" "The restrooms were clean, and the soft and absorbent toilet paper could have stretched for miles!" Geez... don't people have better things to do?

GasBuddy is a great way to save money on fuel in the US. Unfortunately, there doesn't seem to be a GasBuddy equivalent in Europe.

Cheapflights, Momondo, GoEuro, Kayak, Rome2rio, Skyscanner
These apps comprise the Rosetta Stone for deciphering schedules and finding inexpensive transportation. Plane? Train? Automobile? One or more of these apps has you covered. For detailed information about finding transportation, check out the Transportation chapter.

Snapseed

If the smartphone is your only device and you take photos, as practically all travelers do, you're going to need a photo editor. I'll save you the trouble of trying out a bunch of apps yourself. In fact, I test-drove a few and settled on Snapseed because it is easy to use and has a decent arsenal of editing tools. All of the normal tweaks are included: cropping, light adjustment, color adjustment, vignetting, and some filters, and with a budget-acceptable price of free, it's worth the room it takes in memory.

Google Translate

Many people express concern that it will be difficult to travel in a country where they don't know the language. It's a common apprehension, one that has crossed my mind from time to time. Cambodia? I don't speak Cambodian. Even the alphabet is different. Google Translate is just the app to allay those fears. Though point and mime work pretty well, sometimes it's extremely helpful to have the actual words you need to ask for information or to express a thought more clearly. Google Translate has saved our tocino (bacon in Spanish) on more than one occasion.

Although it works best when you have Wi-Fi or cell data service, it can also be used offline. To use the app offline, download the language you want to translate to your phone. Go to the menu, select "Offline translation," and then pick the language(s) that you'll need. By having the language in your phone's memory, you can type a phrase in English and see it in the foreign language. For more popular languages, you can not only see the translation but hear the translation as well.

When you have Wi-Fi or cell data service, the app becomes extremely powerful. The "Camera" option lets you point the camera at a sign or menu to see the translation. Pretty cool! No one likes to order three potato dishes (not that I know anyone who has done that...) and no protein or vegetables. The app has an option that allows you to translate on the fly, but it gets a little dizzying since the words jump around as you move the phone. For best results, turn that option off, and snap a photo of what you want to translate. Boxes appear around words that the app is able to translate. Click on the words in the boxes and you'll see the translation.

Another useful feature is "Conversation." Just as the name implies, you can have a spoken conversation with another person, but Google Translate steps in and acts as the interpreter. Click "Auto" and the app will listen for your language and the other person's language too and translate as you go. Again, this is only available for widely spoken languages such as Spanish, French, etc.

Even when the language you need to be translated isn't a widely spoken one, and Google Translate can't "speak" it, the "Voice" option is still helpful. Instead of typing what you want to say on the phone's keyboard, you can speak what you want to be translated. It's much faster than typing. The translation is then displayed so that you can show the person your question in their own language on your phone. Also, they can speak their response and it will be translated into English. The app has translated all of the languages that we have ever needed to translate. It just can't speak them all.

The final feature is "Handwriting," one that comes in handy when the alphabet is not the Latin alphabet. Use your finger to draw the characters one-by-one and the app will translate.

Skype and Google Hangouts
Skype and Google Hangouts are VOIP services. There are others too, including Facebook Messenger for FB to FB calls. That means that whenever you have a decent data connection, Wi-Fi or cellular, you can make an international phone call. As mentioned earlier, calling from Skype account to Skype account is free. Calling people in the USA and Canada runs a little over 2 cents per minute, but with Google Hangouts you can call the USA and Canada for free from most countries, and other countries for low rates. Be sure to install both Hangouts and the Hangouts Dialer if you plan to use Hangouts for calling phones.

"We took a short hike up a hill to some pretty gardens on our last full day in Nice, but it was probably a bad idea. The next morning, I was full of phlegm and we were

feeling wiped out for our 4hr bus ride to Montpellier. That doesn't sound bad on the surface until you figure in schlepping our bags on, off, and between three public buses in Nice to get to the long-haul bus.

By the time we sat our butts down for the 4hr transit, we were pooped. I hooked the phone up to the bus's Wi-Fi to watch our progress on Google Maps and immediately started dozing. About an hour into the journey, my phone rang. It was the Facebook Messenger phone app. I panicked immediately. The only person who calls with the FB app is my brother, and it was the wee hours of the morning for him.

"Hello. What's up?" I asked as calmly as possible knowing full well this was not going to be good news. "Dad had a stroke," my brother said. "How bad? Is he okay? Where is Mom?" They were all still at the hospital and tests were being run. Information was slowly trickling in. The good news was that they got Dad to the hospital quickly, and it was categorized as a minor stroke, but his speech and mobility were definitely affected. Nothing is minor when you are nearly 90 years old."

Getting News from Home with Facebook's VOIP

Microsoft Surface Pro 3

As I've remarked a few times, Pat is the photographer in the family, and he uses Lightroom and Photoshop for processing photos, so he needs a powerful computer to handle those programs. Fortunately, his Surface Pro 3 is lightweight yet powerful. It is a serious PC with the power and display quality he needs to work his photo magic.

Most travelers won't need this kind of power on the road, but if you are a heavy processing-power user and need the Windows operating system to run your programs, the Microsoft Surface will serve you well. It is expensive, though.

Rosetta Stone

If you plan on spending a lot of time in a single country, you may want to consider studying the language beyond "hello," "thank you," "goodbye," and "beer," of course. I used Rosetta Stone to learn un petit peu (a little bit) of French. I found the lessons to be interesting and the interactive teaching method practically immersive. What I don't like about Rosetta Stone is that they have moved to a subscription-based model where you pay by the month for certain features. That being said, I see that there is a new competitor in the language-learning arena called Ouino. It has quite a few good reviews and is a fraction of the price of Rosetta Stone. I haven't used it, so I can't give a personal recommendation, but you may want to research it if you are in the market for language-learning software.

Google Account

In order to get the most out of the Google apps and devices, you need a Google account. If you purchase a Chromebook or an Android phone, you will be prompted to sign in to your account or to create one if you don't have one. Even if you are using an Apple or Windows device, when you try to save a location to Google Maps, you will be prompted to sign in or to create an account. Other apps have similar requirements, including Google Docs, Google Drive, and Google Keep. By signing up for a Google account, you receive 15 gigabytes of free storage. This is where your map locations, Docs, and other Google app data are stored. You can also use it as a storage location for photos or other files via the Drive app.

Real Camera Equipment

The beautiful photos that you see in many of our blog posts are taken by Pat with serious photo gear. He shoots with a Nikon D7200, has a couple of lenses, a tripod, filters, and a few other odds and ends that not even I am privy to. Anyway, the exact makes and models of the equipment he uses aren't important, although he'd be happy to tell you if you're interested; rather, what matters is how to get the best deal on high-end equipment.

I'm not going to go into what high-end camera gear you should buy, because I honestly have no clue, and I know that very good photographers already have their preferences. Besides, that could be a book in and of itself.

What I will mention, however, is how to save money on the gear you'd like to take on your trip or need to replace before your trip. To that end, Pat discovered a website called Greentoe (sounds gangrenous to me) where you decide how much you want to pay for camera gear. (They broker a few other things in addition to camera gear, by the way.) How Greentoe works is that you go to their website and find the camera, or tripod, or whatever you're interested in buying and select it. When you provide your zip code, Greentoe will show you the lowest online prices, including shipping and tax, and a list of online retailers.

Now the fun begins. You decide how much you want to offer for the equipment. Knock 10%, 20%, or even 30% off the lowest online price, and plug it in. A meter displays the likelihood of your bid being accepted. When you are happy with both the price and your probability of having your bid accepted, click "Continue," and Greentoe will send your offer to their network of certified retailers. These guys are the real deal, and not grey-market merchandise peddlers. If one of the retailers likes your bid, they will sell the equipment to you at your price. Also, if you have technical questions about the equipment, Greentoe will hook you up with an expert to answer your questions. Of course, Pat had some questions prior to a purchase and he was happy with the support he received.

External Hard Drive

As I've mentioned quite a few times, if you don't have your photos in at least two places, you don't have your photos. I store my photos on the super-sized SD card in my smartphone and in the Cloud on Amazon Drive. Pat, on the other hand, can't leave his photos on the camera's SD cards because they are humongous files, and the cards fill up quickly. That's the price he pays for being the Ansel Adams in the family with the fancy DSLR, shooting both jpeg and RAW for every photo (extremely large files that serious photographers prefer but that plebeians can't view).

To make sure Pat's photos have a safe second location, he bought a four-terabyte external drive. It's about the size of a deck of cards and doesn't require an external power source.

His process is to put the camera's SD card into an SD-USB adapter and plug it into the USB port on the Surface. He then downloads the photos to a folder on the Surface. Now the photos are on the SD card AND the Surface, two locations. Next, he copies the photos to the external hard drive. When time permits and the Wi-Fi gods are in a good mood (appropriate sacrifices vary from country to country), he uploads the photos to the Cloud. Of particular note is that he uploads the photos in small batches. The super-huge files he deals with have a much higher incidence of failing to upload than smaller files. Doing a small batch at a time makes it easy to identify the failures and to know which to re-upload. Once the photos are on both the external hard drive and in the Cloud, it is safe for him to remove the photos from the Surface and reformat the SD card to free up memory.

"We met a family while walking down a quiet street one Sunday. They saw that we had a camera and made the international sign for 'take my picture.' Pat obliged them, and then showed them the photo on the camera's screen. We went back into town and had an 8 x 10 print made, and then returned to their house and gave them the picture. They thought it was about the coolest thing in the world. They brought out a couple of chairs for us, plates of food, and mugs of beer. We exchanged stories in our abbreviated Spanish vocabulary and had a very special afternoon. You can't pay for stuff like this!"

Party-Crashing in Salto, Uruguay

Flash Drives

Toss a few flash drives, also known as thumb drives, into your bag. You never know when you might need to print a boarding pass, a visa application, or a ticket but won't have access to a computer with a printer. No worries. Just save the document to the flash drive, head off to a print/photo store, and the document will be printed for you directly from your flash drive. Another reason to pack a few flash drives is that you may want to swap music or photos with a new friend that you've made. Smaller flash drives of around one gigabyte are inexpensive, hold plenty of music or photos, and can be given to your new friend as a gift.

Anker Power Bank

Smartphones, camera batteries, fellow travelers' phones, and other gadgets sometimes run out of juice at the exact wrong time. To make sure we are never stranded, we carry an Anker Power Bank with us. It's a big battery that can fully charge a smartphone many times over before needing to be charged itself. It weighs about 13oz and is 6.5" x 2.3" x 0.9". It has earned the nickname "the brick" for good reason, but it is worth lugging around. When we go walking around cities for a full day, running the GPS takes its toll on the smartphone battery. When we have the brick, though, we never have to worry about the phone dying and us getting hopelessly lost. Be aware, if you are flying, the power bank may not be stowed in your checked bag as incidents of spontaneous combustion have occurred.

Anker Bluetooth Speaker

Ok, this is not essential gear by any stretch of the imagination, but we like our music. When we were traveling through South America ten years ago, that meant an mp3 player and "portable" wired speakers with matching wall-wart (AC-adapter). It was quite the commitment to carry all of that around but, as I said, we like our music. Nowadays, there is no need for an mp3 player, wires, or a wall-wart; instead, we just store our music on our smartphone and wirelessly connect to a ring-box-sized speaker via Bluetooth. It has a rechargeable battery that charges from the same brick or AC charger that charges the smartphone. The sound is pretty good for such a little package, but don't expect ground-shaking bass. If you need more bass, Anker makes a larger speaker with enhanced bass.

Postcards

When you crave a bit of uncertainty in your life, postcards are the ideal foil to the ever-reliable email. Send them home from each country that you visit, and you can play the Did-it-get-there? game with loved ones when you call. I like to call it postal roulette. Drop-ship your friends and family magnets too so that they can display the postal survivors on their refrigerators.

Outlet Strip

This is essential tech to take with you if you have more than one device that needs to be plugged in. How many times has it happened that only one outlet is available in your room, and it is behind the bed or in some other contortion-requiring location? Or, perhaps you are staying in a room in an old building with just one outlet, and the single light source in the room is plugged into it? It's always a tough decision whether to charge your device and sit in the dark or keep the light on and hope your charge will last until you arrive someplace that mercifully has an unoccupied outlet.

If you are traveling internationally, be sure that the strip is rated for 100-240VAC/50-60hz. You also need to ensure that whatever you plug into the outlet strip is rated for the local voltage. DO NOT plug a hairdryer or any other heating device meant for the US into the outlet strip if you are in a country that uses a different voltage/frequency unless you are absolutely certain it is rated for it! The outlet strip does not actually convert the voltage/frequency.

Additionally, some of the better outlet strips for travel have built-in USB charging outlets. Practically everything charges via USB: smartphones, e-readers, wireless speakers, power banks, camera batteries, etc. Another feature to look for is a decent cord length. As I've said, sometimes the only free outlet is behind the bed or a few feet away from a table or nightstand. The outlet strip we dragged around with us had a short and stiff cord, so I can't recommend that particular brand, but this one looks like a winner, the UPWADE Outlet Travel Power Strip. I've put it on my wish list.

12V Charger

If you use a smartphone for navigation when you rent a car, keeping the phone battery charged is imperative. You can always purchase a 12V charger designed for your phone and use the car's 12V outlet (formerly the cigarette lighter for you smokers out there). Or, if you already carry a power bank (a.k.a. brick), keep it well charged and plug into it instead.

Universal AC Adapter

Ok, you have your worldwide-compatible outlet strip, but you still need to plug it into the wall. Outlets in Europe are different from outlets in Asia, which, in turn, are different from outlets in Australia. Some adapters work anywhere in the world while others are region-specific. We bought our adapter in the UK, and I would recommend it, but I can't find it for sale online. In lieu of one identical to ours, I recommend the universal adapter from Xcords based on the specifications and reviews. It is worldwide-compatible, has two USB outlets, and isn't huge.

A Note on Charging USB Devices

Have you ever noticed that sometimes your phone or other gadget seems to charge lickity-split and at other times it seems to take forever when you use the USB port on a computer or outlet strip? There's a reason for that. Not all USB ports are created equal.

There are USB 1.0, USB 2.0, and USB 3.0 ports. Special charging ports may also be available, like on the Anker power bank mentioned above, that can supply even more charging power than any of the USB ports. If you use the wrong one, will you blow up your phone? The good news is that no, you will not blow up your phone or any other USB-chargeable device if you plug it into a high-power port. Your device will only use the amount of current it is designed to use. Will your device charge more quickly if you use the highest power port you can find? Sometimes yes, sometimes no, but if you use a low-power port (USB 1.0, USB2.0) it may charge more slowly, and sometimes it won't charge at all.

Best bet: Use the charger and cable that came with your phone to charge your phone. Phones can be finicky. Don't worry about other devices charging rapidly (Kindle, spare camera battery, Bluetooth speaker, etc.) They can charge while you are out and about, or you can wait to charge them overnight. If you must use a USB port for your phone and you need it charged quickly, use your cable and plug it into the port with the highest power. USB 1.0/2.0 ports are usually black. A USB 3.0 has more power than a USB 1.0 or 2.0 and usually has a blue "tongue." Dedicated charging ports may be labeled with a lightning bolt and will also provide more power.

Guidebooks and Tourist Information

"We walked this way and that and finally realized that we were near a winery, thanks to the magical powers of Google Maps and its feature that allowed us to pre-mark wineries and other points of interest. We walked up to it, but the hours posted there indicated that it was closed for the mid-day siesta, or whatever they call it in France. Still, the winery was photogenic, so Pat made me pose for a photo in front of it. No sooner did Pat snap the photo than the door opened and the winemaker/owner popped his head out and asked if we wanted to taste his wines. What? Who? Us? Try wine? Before you could make the sound of a cork being pulled from a bottle, we said 'Yes!'"

The Start to a Memorable Day in Thuir, France

I love reading guidebooks. Who doesn't, right? My problem is that I tend to read them like novels and get lost in the atmosphere created by the descriptions of the sights, the foods, and the activities. I'll finish reading about a city or town and decide that I'd love to explore it, but almost immediately I'll have forgotten what specific sights, markets, or museums I want to see. I'll also have absolutely no clue where they are in the city or where they are relative to each other. I blame it on being over 50 and having a short attention span.

As always, necessity is the mother of invention. With today's technology and online resources, you have no reason to miss the Michelin-starred Rocky Mountain Oyster restaurant, the Atacama Museum of Umbrellas and Galoshes, or whatever interests you. Doesn't it just bunch your socks when you meet another traveler who visited the same city you did and saw something you would have loved to have seen if only you had known it was there? Or, worse yet, how about when you hear about something great to do or see, and you completely forget about it when you're in that city?

Gone are the days of lugging around a dog-eared guidebook the size of Webster's Unabridged Dictionary. With today's smartphones and easy internet access, you can have unlimited information right in the palm of your hand.

KindleUnlimited

If you are traveling for an extended time to multiple countries or even continents, you can't possibly take all of the guidebooks you would like in paperback form. You'd have one heck of a time packing them all and possibly go broke in the process. KindleUnlimited is a clever solution to having all of the guidebooks you need or want, at a fraction of the cost and weight.

Another advantage is that you don't even need a Kindle to subscribe to the service, though I'd highly recommend one. You can just install the Kindle reader app onto your smartphone or laptop. The advantage of actually having a Kindle is that you can read when you're outdoors in the sunlight. Big plus!

What is KindleUnlimited? It's an Amazon subscription service that gives you access to over a million books in the Amazon library, and it costs about $10/month, which is less than a single guidebook. You can select up to ten titles at any given time and have access to them even when you're offline. Amazingly, many of the Lonely Planet guides are part of the KindleUnlimited library.

Once you are signed up, be sure to install the Kindle app on your smartphone and/or laptop, even if you already have a Kindle. It's convenient to access your books from multiple devices, and the app keeps your reading progress synced across all of them when you have an internet connection. Also, don't forget to move the books to your device's memory so you can read them even when you don't have an internet connection. With your books loaded onto your smartphone, laptop, and/or Kindle, you're all set for a long flight or bus ride, and you'll be well-informed when you arrive at your destination.

Rick Steves' Guidebooks

Rick Steves is the undisputed master of travel in Europe. His books are fantastic and full of details including well-thought-out itineraries. He has been traveling in Europe most of his life, and his enthusiasm shines through. Unfortunately, the Rick Steves' guidebooks aren't a part of the KindleUnlimited library, but you can purchase them through the Kindle store.

Rick Steves has a television series too, and you can find complete episodes on YouTube. It's interesting to watch an episode about a city just before you arrive or even while you're there. If there is a don't-miss sight or activity, Rick will let you know.

Another cool thing that Rick Steves does is Audio Tours. He has recorded commentary to accompany self-guided walking tours in popular cities and famous museums. To find his commentary, search for "Rick Steves Audio Europe" in your app store, install the app on your smartphone, and then download the tour you are interested in taking. It's an informative way to see a city and it's free!

The Lonely Planet Guides

The Lonely Planet guides are packed with information and are the gold standard in parts of the world where Rick Steves doesn't command the stage. Even in Europe, though, they score a solid silver. As mentioned above, many of the Lonely Planet guides are available on KindleUnlimited. Of course, if a certain title isn't available on KindleUnlimited, you can still purchase it.

> *"'Something must have gone wrong for you to be stuck in La Entrada...' This is a direct quote from the Lonely Planet travel-bible. Well, guess what? We left San Salvador promptly, early in the morning. The bus was a bit slow, but it eventually dropped us off in El Poy, El Salvador, from where we walked across the border and then took a short taxi ride to Nueva Ocotepeque, Honduras. The bus from there to La Entrada was late! By the time we got to La Entrada, we had missed the last bus to Copan. We were stuck in La Entrada, and the Hotel Alexandria became our home for the night. Luckily, we found an excellent little restaurant for food and beer. The next morning, we stood by the side of the road and flagged down the first bus labeled 'Copan Ruinas.' It turned out to be one of those fancy-schmancy airplanes on wheels, and we were the only passengers. Sweeeeeeet!"*

La Entrada, Honduras Wasn't So Bad

What I really like about the Lonely Planet guides is that they show where everything is on a map. The offline maps can be a little bit difficult to read on a smartphone, and even on a laptop, but the guides also provide a link to Google Maps when you have an internet connection. This is very handy, and I'll explain why in a moment.

Atlas Obscura

If the offbeat and flat-out weird is what you are seeking in the world, AtlasObscura, the website or the book, is for you. Atlas Obscura digs up unusual attractions that don't always find their way into regular guidebooks. Maybe you're into adventurous eating and drinking. If that's your bag of chips, Atlas Obscura has a new section called Gastro Obscura that focuses on interesting, sometimes challenging, food and drink.

> *"We walked down the 13 flights of stairs to the ground floor. People and things appeared their normal sizes*

*again. Alice in Wonderland would know the feeling. The
lights were hung in such a way as to give the great
cavern an eerie, almost psychedelic atmosphere. A Ferris
wheel? Groovy.*

*There was a large hole at the far end of the cavern.
Peering into the hole revealed a lower level, another ten,
or so, stories down. The floor of the lower cavern was
submerged. A wooden bridge led from the unseen
entrance below us out to a salt island covered in decking.
At various places along the deck were open structures
with spots for people to sit and absorb the restorative salt
air. Odd fluorescent lights decorated and lit the
structures. Trippy.*

*We walked down the narrow stairs to the lake level.
Rowboats scudded phantasmagorically around the lake.
There were a lot of people, yet it was quiet. The hushed
tones were like those in a library or a place of worship.
The people who sat there looked terribly bored, though.
Some played crossword puzzles. Others just stared off
into the darkness. I wondered if they were sent there on
doctor's orders."*

Exploring the Salina Turda Salt Mine in Romania

Google Maps

I must sound like a squeaky windshield wiper rubbing on a
partially dry windshield. Google Maps, Google Maps, Google
Maps. Honestly, I use it for everything. Google Maps is
another great way to discover sights and activities that
interest you. Traveling to Scotland? Search for "distillery."
Going to France? Search for "winery." The travel guides are
great, and you won't miss any major sights (they provide
useful information about history and customs too), but they
are in no way as comprehensive as Google Maps.

Even some guidebooks love Google Maps as much as I do.
Say you are reading through your Lonely Planet guide and
you find a fort that you'd like to see in a city you'll be visiting
in a few weeks. Right from the Kindle app on your
smartphone or laptop, you can click on "Google Maps."

Google Maps will open and show the location of the fort, along with reviews and other information such as its hours of operation and its phone number. You can save the fort to Google Maps with a click of a button. To do so just click "save" and select the star icon. Boom! It's on your map. Now imagine that you are taking a walk in that city. You read the guide weeks ago and saved places of interest to your map. Take a look at Google Maps on your smartphone, and point your feet in the direction of the stars!

When we were in Thailand, for example, I was busy reading the France Lonely Planet guide and marked many things to do and see on Google Maps. I also searched for wineries in the areas where I knew we would be spending a lot of time and marked them on Maps too. By the time we got to France, I had all but forgotten what I had read, but there were stars sprinkled all over my map. If the wineries had not been pre-marked, we would have missed a most amazing day with the winemaker in Thuir.

Google Maps is also an invaluable tool for planning what to explore over a few days since you can see what is close together and group things accordingly. I love Google Maps. Did I mention that yet?

Tourist Information Offices

This is a bit obvious, but tourist information offices are offices that supply tourists with free information (donations are a nice way to say thank you). You can pretty much count on being able to pick up a map, use the bathroom, have lunch at a picnic table, or ask a knowledgeable person questions about public transportation, lodging, specific museums, or notable sights. You just never know what additional things tourist information offices might have.

"We were lost. Sablet was the nearest village, so we went back there to see if we could get directions. The tourist info office was just about to close for lunch, but we caught the woman and asked about Chêne Bleu Winery. She looked at us quizzically and then basically said, 'You can't get there from here.' I hate when that happens. She told us to come back at 3pm when the office reopened. Turns

out, the tourist information office was a wine-tasting room too. I love when that happens!

Obediently, we went away for two hours and found a park for our VinoLunch after which we took a walk through Sablet. At exactly 3pm, we were back at the tourist information office. There were so many wines open for tasting we didn't know which ones to sample. The main grape in Côtes du Rhône is Grenache, but Syrah is grown too and others to a lesser extent. A complex set of rules governs the percentages of each grape that can be used in a Côtes du Rhône AOC wine.

Though the tasting and information were fabulous, we were disappointed that we never found Chêne Bleu, but we were ecstatic to learn that tourist information offices in the Vaison Ventoux region were also tasting rooms."

Finding WIne-Tasting in Tourist Information Offices in the Vaison Ventoux Region of France

Airbnb Experiences

Experiences are a relatively new offering from Airbnb. Not only can you find a room through Airbnb, but you can book unique experiences with locals. For example, in Florence, Italy, there are numerous photography experiences such as classes, walks, and shoots. Florence is a stunningly photogenic city, after all. Other common experiences are food tours, wine tastings, yoga, and cooking classes. You might even find a "How to Hunt for Truffles" experience.

Local Knowledge

Don't forget to ask your host and other locals about what is special about their town. Need a recommendation for a relaxing park for a picnic lunch? Ask a local, and don't forget to mark its location on your map. Keep your ears tuned to what others are talking about in restaurants and bars. I don't mean eavesdrop on intimate conversations, but if you hear someone ask the bartender if he's going to the Upton Blues Festival this weekend, and you like blues music, you might want to jot that down. Google it when you have a chance, or ask the bartender about it if he has time.

> *"So how did two Americans get to this small town in the middle of rural England, one that was hosting such a big event? Pubs! For centuries they have been places of information exchange, and they are still. We spent a good deal of time at the Chase Inn, which was located near our pet-sitting gig, downing a few pints and chowing on lovely fish and chips. During the course of conversation — drinking real ale and conversation go hand in hand — we were told of this amazing blues festival and that it was only seven miles away. Even a Yankee like me can handle that short of a drive, although I didn't take into account that thousands of other people would be scrambling to get to the same place at the same time. Actually, getting there wasn't all that bad, and we were able to find a parking spot within a half mile of the town. Muddy Waters must have blessed the event because the weather was spectacular, which lent itself well to inhaling more pints of real ale, consuming pub food, and dancing in the streets."*

Finding the Blues in Upton-on-Severn, England

Traveler Knowledge

Along the lines of local knowledge is traveler knowledge. Other travelers are a great source for recommending sights and experiences. Thinking about taking the bus from Coroico to Rurrenabaque, Bolivia, to see the Amazon River Basin? Ask other travelers if they have done it and what it was like. Was the Amazon River Basin tour even worth doing? (It was, by the way.)

> *"There are two ways to get to Rurrenabaque, Bolivia. The first way is to hop onto a really crappy bus in Coroico and take really crappy and scary roads for approximately 20-24 hours. The second way is to take a minivan back to La Paz, up the new Death Road, and catch a flight to Rurrenabaque. After asking around and hearing from quite a few 20-somethings that they would*

NEVER, NEVER, EVER do the bus ride again, we smarter, older folk opted for the airplane. Good choice!"

Getting to the Amazon River Basin in Bolivia

Travel Blogs

Both amateur and professional travel blogs are also great sources of information and inspiration. My favorite travel blog is VinoHiking.com. Ok, that's cheap self-promotion, but, hey, it's not beneath me. Anyway, Pat and I have written about our travels in over 40 countries and have tried to keep the stories fun and insightful, with some useful tips thrown in for good measure. I hope you check it out.

It is difficult to provide a list of recommended travel blogs because they are best when they are fresh. An easy way to find travel bloggers, though, is to search Facebook and Twitter for "travel." Examples of blogs that I have followed over the past year or so on Facebook include the following: Roaming Around the World, by a young couple who completed a trip around the world without flying; Rip to the Tip, by a couple riding motorcycles in Africa; Motoroaming, by a fun couple that we met in Bulgaria, who were traveling through Europe in a motorhome. On Twitter, Richard Barrow in Thailand covers Thailand, and Pakse Cafe has information on all parts of Southeast Asia. Many times, people commenting on travel blogs are travel bloggers themselves. Check them out too.

Posters, Brochures, Billboards, etc.

Keep your eyes open! Food fairs, concerts, art walks, and the like are often advertised on a banner, on a poster, on a billboard, or in a local events brochure. Some cities even have free weekly papers that highlight live entertainment and food and beverage festivals. In Canoa, Ecuador, we learned of a surfing competition from a poster on a bus. In Lima, Peru, we saw a banner promoting a food festival. In Baja, Mexico, banners touting the Baja 500 criss-crossed the streets of Ensenada. Chili cook-offs, car shows, free concerts, wine festivals, and more happen all of the time.

Small local events can be a lot of fun and are a great way to learn more about the people and their culture.

> "We found a small brochure in our Sofia, Bulgaria, Airbnb apartment that listed events taking place over the summer. For example, a jazz festival, A to JAZZ, was going on in the park. Cool! But no mention was made of where to buy tickets as far as I could tell. Then again, Bulgarian is not my strong suit. I tracked the organizers down on Facebook and sent them a message. 'How much are tickets? Where can we buy them? Can we bring a backpack to the venue? Our own food and drinks?' On the off-chance of a positive response, I added: 'Can we bring wine?'
>
> A short while later, I received a response, 'You can bring everything you want. The entrance is free for all three days.' I gave them two thumbs up, which they obviously couldn't see, and said, 'Dobre! Dobre!' which they obviously didn't hear."

Finding a Great Jazz Festival in Sofia, Bulgaria

Gear

"After a few photos of absolutely breathtaking scenery, we hopped back into the Land Rover and started bouncing our way down into the valley. I really do mean bounce. Our bags were doing doh-si-dohs above my head on the roof, I swear. I thought for sure they were going to break the bungee cord, leap off the roof, and sink to the bottom of a pothole never to be seen again. Maybe that would have been a good thing for subsequent vehicles as the pothole would at last be filled, but, on the negative side, we'd be running around buck naked on laundry day."

Dropping into Theth, Albania - Everything We Owned Was in Those Bags

When it comes to what gear to take on your trip, certain things can help make your journey easier, more comfortable, and even less expensive, and there are certain items we never travel without.

Gear for Eating

We picnic... a lot. It's an enjoyable way to have a meal, and it's also cost-effective. That's why we pack our own plastic plates and utensils. But, why wouldn't you just use the plates and utensils from your accommodation? You can, but sometimes your accommodation won't have a kitchen, or you might be traveling between accommodations when mealtime arrives. Besides, you never know what will be provided. If you're going on a VinoHike, you don't want to lug plates and bowls around that weigh as much as reinforced concrete. The wine bottle is heavy enough.

Folding Dishes and Bowls
Folding plastic dishes and bowls make picnicking easy. They take up nearly zero room in your bag, and they weigh almost nothing. Besides, have you ever purchased olives at a Greek market? Well, they don't come in a fancy little jar. They come in a plastic bag. Not ideal for serving because the bag tends to fall over and the juice runs everywhere. Stick the bag in a bowl instead, open it up, and enjoy the olives. The bowl gives the bag support, and you don't wind up sitting in a puddle of olive juice.

Another great feature is that the bowls can handle hot water. That means that if you are caught needing to prepare your package of emergency ramen, you can drop the noodles in the bowl, add the seasoning as well as some veggies and/or protein, and then pour on the noodle-softening hot water. Finally, cover the bowl with a plate for about five minutes. Voilà! Memories of college and enough sustenance until morning.

When we travel, we carry two sets of folding plates and bowls, one set for each of us. The sets are made by Fozzils, and they have held up well over the past year.

Utensils
OK, so you packed your plates and bowls and have picked up a jar of anchovies and a baguette in Collioure, France. You are seated on the perfect bench with the perfect view, an ideal spot at which to savor those fishy little rascals along with a lovely bottle of Banyuls wine. Although it's possible to retrieve the anchovies from the jar with your fingers, it's a messy operation. Trust me. I've been there, and wiping your hands on a newspaper doesn't work well either. Save yourself the fishy, greasy, newsprint-stained fingers, and pack some utensils because there's nothing like the aroma

of anchovies to endear you to a bus full of people. A spork is ideal.

Knife and Cutting Board
Apples, dried salami, and aged cheese are all wonderful picnic items, but you'll need a knife if you don't want to gnaw on them whole. Pack a sharp folding knife and a small cutting board, one that fits into your daypack easily, so that slicing up the goodies isn't a digit-threatening affair. If you're traveling by airplane, remember to put your knife in your checked bag, or wait until you arrive at your destination and buy a knife there. The cutting board isn't absolutely necessary if you have the folding plates and bowls, but plastic plates and bowls aren't as rigid as a cutting board, and the thinner plastic of the plates and bowls will last much longer if you don't cut on it.

Can Opener
Don't wind up with a can without a pull-top and no way to open it. If you think all sardine tins have a pull-top, you'd be wrong... and hungry, if that was all you packed for your picnic. The spork set mentioned above comes with a micro-can/bottle opener. Our can opener is a cheap regulation-size can opener which is much easier to use than the compact opener, though bulkier.

Zipper Bags
Resealable zipper bags are worth much more than their weight in gold. They have many uses and are so light and easy to pack that you might as well take some along. I like to have a few gallon-sized bags and six or so quart-sized bags. As the following list shows, they can perform a wide array of functions.

- Did you make too much food for dinner, but there aren't any storage containers at your Airbnb? Quart-sized bags are perfect.
- Need to make ice for your afternoon Pastis, but there's no ice tray? Fill a zipper bag with water, not too full, and freeze it. Wrap the bag of frozen water in a towel and whack it with a saucepan or the butt

of a knife. The bag may not survive, but who wants warm Pastis?

- Need an ice-pack for a sore knee or a bump on your head? Freeze 1 part rubbing alcohol (I suppose vodka could work too, and you can drink it when you're done) and 2 parts water in a zipper bag to make a gel ice pack.
- Have messy leftovers from your VinoHike that you fear will dirty the inside of your daypack? Keep a quart bag in your pack, and stick the nasty items in there until you can dispose of them.
- Stuck without a pillow? Lightly inflate a gallon bag and slip a t-shirt over it. (Or, roll up a sweater like a normal person.)
- Need to keep your passport or other documents dry? Put them in a quart bag, and then stow it in your money belt or bag.
- Want to take photos on your kayak trip with your phone? Place your phone in a new zipper bag, one that isn't hopelessly wrinkled, and zip it up. You can operate the phone and take pictures through the bag. Ok, the photos aren't going to be studio-quality, but they will be serviceable for a Facebook or blog post, and you won't ruin your phone if you drop it in the water.
- Need to pack wet or olfactory-challenging clothing? Put your bathing suit, smelly socks, or whatever, into a zipper bag and thereby keep the rest of your clothes dry and odor-free.
- Flying? The TSA requires that your carry-on liquids be in containers of no more than 100ml and all placed in a single quart zipper bag.

News flash: You can wash zipper bags! We used the same bags for nearly a year before they sprung leaks or had been used for something too gross to reuse them. The double-zipper freezer bags hold up better than the cheap sandwich bags. Pack them. You'll use them... and want to thank me with gifts of wine.

A "Tablecloth"

This is one of my favorite items. It isn't something that is packed ahead of time, but something found during the journey. On our last trip, we found a dish towel with a map of Italy on it depicting various Italian foods and wines in their proper regions. Whenever we went out for a picnic, we spread the dish towel on the grass, or park bench, or whatever, and set our goodies on it. As we tasted different wines from different regions in Italy, we put a drop of the wine next to its name on the dish towel. The towel is quite stained and a little nasty at this point, but I don't have the heart to wash it.

> *"It's not a proper outing without a picnic and a bottle of wine. We left the Turda salt mine and found a public park a few blocks away. Per SOP we covered the park bench with our 'tablecloth,' a dish towel we had picked up in Italy, popped open a bottle of Romanian wine, and set out our snacks. It was a beautiful day in a small but pleasant park."*

Relaxing in a Park after Exploring the Salina Turda Salt Mine in Romania

Pantry Items

Will you be doing most of your own cooking? It's convenient to have some basic pantry items. Although the Airbnb description may include a "well-stocked kitchen," different hosts have different ideas of what a well-stocked kitchen is. Two forks, two spoons, two bowls, and two plates constituted "well-stocked" at one Airbnb where at least washing up after a meal was a snap.

As we needed items, we picked them up and schlepped them along in our reusable grocery bag from place to place. Here is what we found we needed:

- Salt
- Pepper
- Hot sauce (no true Arizonan can live without it)
- Oil
- Vinegar
- Tea bags

- Instant coffee (Yuck, I know, but you can always make hot water. Coffee makers aren't a given.)
- Emergency ramen
- Paper towels

Yes, emergency ramen is a thing, and it has been a lifesaver on a few occasions. In Blaenau Ffestiniog, Wales, (spell that five times fast) nearly 100% of our daily budget went toward our room, and the restaurants in town were wallet-suckers. Hot water was free, the ramen and the veggies were cheap, and we averted a loan application by going a-la-broke-backpacker and eating our noodles. Another time, in Perpignan, France, we were caught off-guard by a holiday (I swear that every other day is a holiday in France), and all of the markets and restaurants were closed. Thanks to the emergency ramen that we carted around, we didn't have to resort to cannibalism or thinning the rather large feral cat population.

Gear for Drinking

Yes, eating is important, but drinking is too. As VinoHikers, and partakers of potent potables, we have experimented with countless different vessels for liquids and found what works best. Mind you, none of the testing was an imposition at all.

Cup

That sounds simple, doesn't it? Well, we have tried all kinds of plastic glasses (Plastic glass? Is that oxymoronic like jumbo shrimp?) and have found that a plastic stackable cup is the best and most versatile option. We tried plastic wine glasses with screw-off stems, but they took too much room, and their mortal sin was that they were easy to knock over. Stemless Govino wine glasses were our next goblet of choice, but they also took up too much room, weren't very sturdy, and were easy to crack. What works best are stackable plastic cups. They have a low center of gravity and a wide bottom, so they're less likely to spill than a plastic glass with a stem. They are much more durable than Govino stemless plastic glasses too, of which I have cracked a few.

Another benefit is that the plastic cups stack, making them easy to pack. They work just fine for water, wine, or scotch on the rocks, and they can even hold hot liquids and foods (instant oatmeal, for one).

Make sure, though, that the cup is BPA-free so that odors do not permeate it and that chemicals do not leach out of it and into your food or drink. The only drawback with plastic cups is that I haven't been able to find a colorless, clear one so that I can see my wine better. Drop me a line if you find one.

"Water, water everywhere and all of it good to drink. Glaciers have rivers and pools of water throughout them. No need to carry bottles of water; just take an empty cup and dip in when you get thirsty."

Hiking on the Perito Moreno Glacier in Argentina

Collapsible Flask

Do you plan on backpacking? Buying wine by the liter? Smuggling booze onto a cruise ship? Or, just enjoying a scotch on the rocks in the evening? If you answered yes to any of these questions, you need at least one Collapsible Flask.

When you are backpacking, keeping your pack light is of the utmost importance, and having something to nip on in the tent is right up there too. Ditch the bottle and fill a flask. A collapsible flask is much lighter than a bottle and just as leakproof, but beware of spiny flora! On our second day backpacking in the Torres del Paine National Park in Chile, I set my backpack down to take a rest. Unfortunately, I didn't realize it then, but a thorn had poked right through my backpack and into the flask. Needless to say, we were extremely disappointed when we got into camp and discovered that our flask was empty. Pat and I drew straws to determine who got to suck on my scotch-soaked backpack.

Besides being lightweight, collapsible flasks can also perform another vital function. In France and Italy, we came across wine co-ops and vino sfuso, respectively. They are the bastions of all that is right in the world. You take an empty bottle, jug, jerrycan, or collapsible flask, fill it with wine and then pay (at a greatly reduced rate) by the liter. It brings a tear to my eye just thinking about it.

> *"We sat there on our bench, nibbling on snacks and sipping wine (we are professionals, but feel free to try this at home), fresh focaccia with onions, olives, fried anchovies, and Nebbiolo from our newest, best friend, Mr. Vino. Mr. Vino was our Genovese wine hook-up. He does Vino Sfuso (wine by the liter) and has a large selection of red and white wines. We sampled a few of them, then settled on the Nebbiolo as our staple."*

Buying Wine by the Liter in Genoa, Italy

Even if you aren't a wino but prefer a beverage with a little more giddy-up instead, a collapsible flask will help you too. As everyone knows, buying in bulk saves money, and liquor is no exception. The problem with buying a one-liter or a 1.75-liter bottle, though, is that it takes a while to finish one off. Instead of hauling the equivalent of a few more cocktails-worth of liquor around in a big heavy bottle, pour the remainder into a collapsible flask. Your back will thank you, and your bag will heave a sigh of relief... your liver might have something else to say, though.

And, as a final note on collapsible flasks, most cruise ships forbid you to bring more than a couple of bottles of wine on board, and if they do, you might have to pay a steep corkage fee in order to drink your wine. Liquor, on the other hand, is never permitted. Now, I'm not suggesting that you do anything against the cruise line's policies, but drinks on cruise ships are stinking expensive!

> *"[S]muggling liquid contraband on board is difficult. I probably shouldn't tell you this, but we did manage to sneak some aboard. I won't tell you how, in case we need to do it again, but I will say that Carrie was in a motherly way briefly. As a matter of fact, she nearly 'delivered' while going through the ship's security, as the 'baby'*

began to descend, but she did manage to get through the scanner and waddle down the hall to find a secluded spot to give 'birth'."

Bottle Opener

Whether you like a cold brew or a Cab Sauvignon, you need to open it if you're going to drink it, so don't forget your corkscrew/bottle opener, but be careful. If you fly and the TSA is involved, make sure your wine opener doesn't have a foil cutter, or else make certain that it is stowed in your checked bag. If not, the TSA agent will unceremoniously steal your wine opener and dispose of it right before your very eyes. The particular agent who stole my gift from lovely wine shop owners in Ljubljana, Slovenia, wouldn't even let me attempt to break the foil cutter off. What a d^@k. I'm still peeved about this. Can you tell?

Wine Aerator

If you are touring wine country, like we did through France in 2017, you should seriously consider packing a wine aerator. You don't even have to be a wine snob to really come to love this gadget. Any wine-lover, even wine-liker, knows that sometimes a wine needs to "open" before its true flavors come out.

"The man in the shop told us about the wines and helped us pick a couple of bottles aligned with our palate. The main grapes were merlot, cabernet franc, cabernet sauvignon, malbec, and petit verdot. These are a few of my favorite things.

The shop closed up on our heels, so we took to ambling through the narrow cobblestone chemins. We passed fancy wine shops selling library wine selections for thousands of dollars, restaurants with foie gras on the menu, and high-end jewelry and clothing shops. Tourists were everywhere. It was quite a different experience from laid-back and non-touristy Fronsac.

At the top of the hill, we found a stone picnic table overlooking the old stone buildings of Saint-émilion below. It was the perfect spot for a VinoLunch, so we sat down and enjoyed our snacks and a fabulous bottle of Saint-émilion merlot-cabernet franc. Be mindful, once the bottle is opened these wines can take a while to 'breathe' before developing their complex flavors and aromas. We did the old pour-it-back-and-forth-between-glasses a few times to aerate the wine, and it worked out perfectly. We were either lucky or Bacchus was looking out for us because no dribblage occurred. A good day was had by all."

Aerating Wine the Old-School Way - Saint-émilion, France

Hydration Bladder or Reusable Bottle

Believe it or not, we drink water too. Staying hydrated is important for feeling well and alert. If you do a lot of hiking, a hydration bladder is a convenient way to drink water while you trek. It is a one- to two-liter plastic bladder with a hose connected to a bite-valve. The bite-valve prevents the water from running out of the hose until you bite on it. You wear the bladder on your back and clip the bite-valve to your front. When you feel parched, bite the bite-valve and sip the water. Release the valve, and the flow will stop.

A reusable water bottle is all you need if you do a lot of sitting on buses or make short walks to park benches instead of embarking on hikes or treks. Reusable water bottles have advantages over hydration bladders too. A water bottle can stand on its own, is less expensive, and is infinitely easier to clean. Or, if you have an empty collapsible flask, you can fill it with water and take that with you.

In countries where potable water doesn't come out of the taps, you may have to resort to the dreaded plastic-bottled water. Hang on to the plastic bottle after you empty it, though, because some hostels, guesthouses, and even hotels have purified-water filling-stations. Refill the plastic bottle as many times as you can before buying another, and be sure to recycle it, if possible.

Gear for Lugging

Roller bag? Backpack? Duffle bag? Suitcase? Steamer trunk? Ok, probably not a steamer trunk, but choosing how to carry what you take on your trip is an important decision. For the most part, you will carry a main bag and a "personal item." What is best for you really depends on your mode of travel. Are you flying from city to city? Taking a cruise ship? Mainly riding trains? Renting a car? Some modes of transportation let you spread out a little more than others, but traveling light is always advantageous.

Main Bag

For our style of travel and physical abilities, a convertible bag works best. Our eBags TLS Mother Lode Weekenders have served us well over the past few years, and they have many more years of life left in them. The Mother Lode can be carried like a regular soft-sided suitcase by a handle, or over the shoulder with a shoulder strap, or on the back like a backpack. That's why it's called a convertible. It is also legal carry-on size (if the gusset isn't unzipped and the front pocket isn't stuffed). Keep in mind that in Europe and Asia it is usual that a carry-on must meet certain weight restrictions too. If you aren't flying, no worries!

Why it works for us: It is lighter than a roller bag of the same dimensions because it doesn't have wheels or a telescoping-handle, just a few straps. Also, it can easily tackle any terrain if you put it on your back or over your shoulder. A roller bag, in contrast, needs to be carried when you hit a cobblestone street, a gravel driveway, or a set of stairs. Further, both of your hands remain free when it is on your back or over your shoulder, leaving you the ability to handle tickets and money, look at maps, or use your phone. It can also be stowed in an overhead compartment on an airplane, thus saving you significant checked bag fees.

Packing Cubes

Okay, I didn't always travel like an adult. Way back when we started doing extended land travel, I used a backpack (external frame at that), and rolled my clothes, then stuffed them into stuff sacks. Anything that wasn't polyester was extremely wrinkled, and it was nearly impossible to find a specific shirt without pulling all of the shirts out of the stuff sack. Rolling and stuffing were space-efficient, but very irritating.

Then I found packing cubes. They changed my life. My acne cleared up. I lost weight. Solving the Sunday edition of the New York Times crossword puzzle became a breeze. I may be exaggerating a bit, but packing cubes did change the way I pack... and unpack.

The cubes I use are made by the same company that makes my main bag, eBags. They are designed to fit the main bag efficiently, and many different sizes are available to fit whatever I need to pack. Currently, I use three medium packing cubes (the TLS Mother Lode Weekender can hold four). One cube is for shirts, one for pants and shorts, and the third for socks/underwear/swimsuit. The space left in the main bag where the fourth cube could go is used for my outerwear and sweaters.

So why is this so life-altering? For a start, it keeps clothes well-stowed and organized. I'm not going to promise wrinkle-free clothes, but the clothes do stay fairly neat. If you are a die-hard clothing-roller, though, you can roll your clothes, and they will fit just fine that way too. The best part is that cubes are a snap to unpack. Just take the cubes out, unzip them, and plop the cubes of clothes in a drawer. It sure is easier and a lot more adult-like not having to live out of a suitcase.

Hanging Toiletry Kit
The key to a good toiletry kit is a large, sturdy hook. I can't count the number of tiny bathrooms with zero counter space that we have been in. Where do you set your stuff? Close the toilet lid and set your toothbrush there? Ewww, no! All you need to do to provide a hygienic location on which to set your toothbrush is to make sure your toiletry bag has a sturdy, large hook. You can then hang your toiletry bag from a towel rack, a light fixture, or even a shower curtain ring and confidently slip your toothbrush into one of the pockets and not have to worry about where someone else's sweaty

bum has been. All of your other toiletries will be easily accessible too.

Secondary Bag
Whether you travel by plane, train, bus, or rickshaw, you will most likely carry a secondary bag, sometimes referred to as a "personal item" by the airlines. This is the bag that stays with you at all times and contains your valuables such as your laptop or tablet, your camera, your e-reader, or your tickets. Your main bag, then, may be stowed in a hold or strapped to a roof.

A crossbody sling bag is ideal. It goes across the front of your body so you have easy access to its contents and can keep an eye on it at all times. Also, it doesn't interfere with putting your main bag on your back. Tip: If you wear your main bag on your back, put the sling bag on before your main bag since you'll ditch the main bag first. I almost strangled myself once trying to take my main bag off when I did it the other way around. It wasn't the most graceful maneuver.

When you are traveling by overnight bus, or you decide to take a nap on a plane, wear the sling bag around your neck and put it in your lap, and then cover yourself with a jacket or a blanket. Would-be thieves will look for an easier target than a purse-clutching mummy.

Daypack
I pack a daypack inside my main bag. Hiking is something we do frequently, and having a daypack for our snacks, wine, jackets, water, and other hiking necessities is essential. The daypack also doubles as a shopping bag. When we go to the market or grocery store to buy food for the week, we fill up the daypack with the heavy stuff and put the lightweight groceries in the reusable grocery bag. It sure simplifies hauling groceries many blocks and up stairs.

Only two wine stores came up. One, Halewood, had good reviews. "How far is it?" asked Pat. "Not far, but we should go early," I replied nonchalantly. He knew that that was darn near a fib. 2.5km is nothing, unless the day is hotter than a habanero suppository, which it was. Pat did the scowl-thing. I plotted our course.

We showed up at Halewood bright and early the next morning soaked through like Kleenex in a steam room. It was going to be a ghost pepper kind of day.

Since we had arrived early, we had the shopkeeper to ourselves. He told us about the wines of the region and based on his descriptions, we picked a Feteasca Negra and a red blend. We also mentioned that we were curious about the whites and he asked, almost incredulously, maybe because normal people were just finishing their Cheerios, "You want to taste?" Has a sillier question ever been asked? Of course we wanted to taste!

He poured us handsome portions of the wines we had purchased and then a Feteasca Alba, a white. Ok, wrong tasting order, but we were in a good mood, and nearly perspiration free, by the time we got to the white. "We'll take one of those too!" My back and backpack gave me the evil eye and let me hear about it all the way back to our room.

Hauling More Bottles of Wine than Recommended in My Daypack

Camera Bags

Yes, plural. Pat, like a would-be National Geographic photojournalist, carries one DSLR camera body, two lenses, a tripod, a Surface Pro 3 laptop, filters, spare batteries, a battery charger, various cables, and things that I have no idea what they are. It's a lot of gear, and heavy too, but he is able to fit it all into a backpack-style camera bag and carry it comfortably (if you are wondering, he carries his main bag by the handle or with the strap over his shoulder). Being able to carry the camera bag on his back makes it easy for him to navigate airports, bus stations, train stations, and the like.

When he goes out for a hike or a walk in a city, though, he doesn't necessarily want to take all of his gear. That's why he packs a smaller sling-style camera bag inside his main travel bag. The camera (with lens attached), the second lens, and a few filters and other things fit inside the smaller camera bag. The tripod straps to the outside. The bag has a quick-draw compartment which gives him easy access to the camera, so he is always ready to snap a shot. The bag also has a built-in rain cover ensuring that even the weather can't thwart his efforts to capture a scene.

Money Belt

Oh, yes. The old money belt. I know you hear people say that they don't wear a money belt because all thieves know that tourists are likely to be wearing one. Despite this, I never travel without mine. I mean, what is a thief more likely to infiltrate, your purse/daypack or the smelly sweaty money belt from which even you can't extricate your passport without spraining your wrist? It doesn't matter if the thief knows you are wearing one. He or she is not going to go after your money belt when the guy standing next to you has his wallet in his back pocket.

To keep our money and IDs safe, we put only the cash we think we'll need for the day into our wallets along with one of our credit cards (each of us uses a different one), or a debit card if we need to hit an ATM. Our wallets go into the front pockets of our pants and we never set them down on a table or counter. The rest of the cash, additional credit cards, debit cards, driver's licenses, and our passports go into our money belts. As a further precaution, our money belts block RFID transmissions, preventing techy thieves from scanning our credit cards or IDs.

But what if you need to take something out of your money belt when people are around? Don't worry about it. Just pull your money belt up and out of the waistband of your pants, take what you need and put it back. It's really not a secret. It's just a nearly impossible place for a thief to break into. What if you typically wear a dress? Luckily, they make neck wallets too. It's my opinion that they are an easier target than a traditional money belt because someone can cut the neck strap if they are able to see it and wait for the wallet to fall out of the bottom of your dress. It's better than nothing, though.

At the end of the day, when you are back at your room, you should have a routine for what you do with your money belt when you take it off. I always wrap mine up with its strap and stuff it into the same location in one of my bags. It's a heart-pumping experience forgetting where you stashed your money belt, especially when you came up with a clever spot to hide it and you have only a few minutes to catch your bus.

Also, avoid using the in-room safe in your hotel. Your money belt may or may not be more secure in it, but if using it isn't part of your routine, you are apt to forget about it when you check out. Tip: To keep hotel staff from rummaging through your stuff, lock the in-room safe with nothing in it. They will assume that all of your valuables are stowed in it.

P.S. Don't forget to wash your money belt from time to time. Belly-sweat is not the most pleasant fragrance after a while.

Reusable Grocery Bag

A lot of countries in Europe have already done away with plastic and paper grocery bags. It is often part of the culture for locals to take a reusable bag or even a cart to the store. In countries where they still pack your order in a plastic bag, it's environmentally friendly to refuse the plastic and to use your own bag instead.

When the reusable bag is not being used for grocery shopping, it can be used for items that don't fit in your main bag or secondary bag: oil, vinegar, real-sized shampoo, a roll of paper towels, a few packages of ramen, etc. If you are traveling by bus or train, or renting a car, it is little to no problem to carry an extra bag.

Laundry Bag (a.k.a. Stuff Sack)

What about dirty clothes? I'm sure you don't want to put your stinky hiking socks back in your packing cube with your clean socks and undies. That's why a stuff sack makes an ideal laundry bag.

First of all, when it is empty, it is feather-light and takes up just a breath of space. As your clothes move from your packing cubes to the stuff sack, room in your bag naturally opens up to accommodate the laundry bag. Fold the dirty clothes. It is much more efficient than jamming them into a wad.

Second, if you use a laundromat, or if you have someone do your laundry, the stuff sack is a convenient way to transport your clothes to and from the laundromat. By the way, on a related note, having your clothes done for you isn't an extravagance in many parts of the world, like Asia and Central America. Mark your stuff sack with your name in permanent marker, and if you really want to make sure that all of your clothes are returned, write your name in your clothes too.

Other Handy Items

Other useful items include the following:

Towel and Sheet

If you use hostels, or go backpacking, or wind up in an Airbnb without sheets and towels, a quick-dry towel and a camp sheet are worth packing. They are invaluable if you need them and only a small addition to your bag if you never use them. Who wants to sleep directly on a hostel mattress or in a rented sleeping bag without a clean sheet between your body and it? Also, not having a towel and drying off with a t-shirt is no fun. Besides, it takes a t-shirt a long time to dry.

Though we rarely use our sheets and towels, we are relieved to have them when we need them. Once, in Montpellier, France, we arrived at our incense-scented Airbnb to find no linens, but a rather healthy cannabis plant, for what it's worth. I normally don't book rooms that provide a cannabis plant in lieu of sheets and towels, but the French description didn't translate well enough into English for me to discern that important bit of information. Thankfully, we had our own linens.

TP and Hand Sanitizer

Need I say more? Throw a good length of toilet paper and a travel-sized bottle of hand sanitizer into a zipper bag and stow it in your purse or daypack. These are definitely items that you will be relieved to have after you've relieved yourself and realize that the TP dispenser has already been relieved of its entire roll.

Permanent Marker
As mentioned in the Laundry Bag section, it is a good idea to write your name on your laundry bag and clothes if you are having them washed by someone else. A permanent marker can also be used to mark your bag of food or cans or bottles in a communal refrigerator. If you have used one of your zipper bags for something a little nasty and you don't want to put food items in it next time, make a note on it in permanent marker. A permanent marker can be fun too. Sometimes a hostel or guesthouse will have a wall where they invite guests to draw something or write their names.

Business Cards
What? I'm on a sabbatical! Exactly. You are going to meet fantastic people along the way, and you will want to keep in touch with them. Sticky notes with an email address become lost. A paper napkin with a phone number scrawled on it quickly deteriorates into a pile of fluff, but business cards... business cards are sturdy and are always put safely into a wallet.

A little over a year ago, we ordered 500 cards from Vistaprint (very inexpensively) and have handed out all but maybe 50 of them. What's more, people love them and there is no doubt that there are a few people with whom we would have otherwise lost contact if it weren't for the card.

So, what do you put on a non-business business card? Our card is pretty innocuous. It has the URL of our travel blog, the name of our Facebook page, our first and last names, our home city, state, and country, our email addresses, the VinoHiking logo (you can put your photo if you like), and our motto: Hike Drink Live Laugh.

On the other hand, we do not include our home address because although we may have hit it off with someone, we really don't know them. Our telephone number isn't on the card either, not because we think we'll receive spam calls, but because Verizon won't let us suspend our phone number for as long as we go away. Each time we come back,

Verizon has given away our phone number and assigns us a new one. I don't even know my phone number anymore.

Making the cards was a holdover from our cruising days. Cruisers make boat-cards and hand them out like Owsley tabs at Woodstock. No one ever remembers people's names, just the boat's name. To this day, we still call cruising friends by their boat name - the Loonies, the Slip Aways,... It was great fun collecting boat cards too. I wish more land-travelers would pick up the idea.

Day Planner

Technology can fail. Smartphones can be stolen. Having the address of your next lodging and its phone number written down on paper provides peace of mind. I use a day planner for that reason and to keep a rudimentary diary of what we saw and did each day. Reading through the entries is a great way to jog my memory when I go to write a blog post, and it's entertaining to read through old day planners years after a trip. Also, I previously kept track of our daily expenses in a day planner, but now Pat puts our expenses directly into a spreadsheet.

Shaving Soap and Brush

This one is for the men. Do you want to know what women think is super-sexy — a bare-chested man slathering soapy shave cream on his face with a fine bristle brush. Ooh la la! On top of it being sexy, shaving soap is much more convenient than a can of shaving cream. It packs small and lasts a dog's age. It can even go through a TSA screening in your carry-on bag without worry.

Pat wants me to mention that instead of using after-shave, he uses Eucerin to calm his freshly-shorn face. A little bit goes a long way. He squirts some into a 100ml bottle (TSA-legal) and it lasts him a year. Okay, he doesn't shave every day, but it lasts a lot longer than a larger bottle of after-shave.

While we are on the subject of shaving, if you use an electric shaver, make sure you can charge your shaver where you are going. Double-check that it can handle the voltage and frequency of the country you are visiting.

118

Nail Clippers
You probably already thought of these, but this is just a reminder not to forget your nail clippers. Fingernails and toenails continue to grow even in foreign countries. The little fold-out nail file thingy? A TSA agent asked me to snap mine off once. Why wasn't I allowed to snap the foil-cutter off of my wine opener, if that's the case? I'm not fond of the TSA.

First Aid Kit
No one plans on becoming sick or injured while traveling, so packing a first aid kit is something that easily slips through the cracks. A basic kit makes all the difference when you aren't feeling well, though. If you have the runs or feel a UTI coming on, the last thing you want to do is walk a mile to the drugstore. Suggested items include the following:

- Aspirin for headaches, fever reduction, aches, and pains
- Advil (ibuprofin) for muscle soreness, cramps, and reducing inflammation (sprains, strains, etc.)
- Azo for relieving pain associated with a UTI (urinary tract infection)
- Benadryl (diphenhydramine) for allergies
- Prescription meds (have a copy of your prescription with you)
- Sunscreen
- Motion sickness pills, if you are susceptible to motion sickness
- Malaria medication, if you will be traveling in an area where malaria is prevalent
- Imodium (loperamide) for the traveler's trots (diarrhea)
- Pepto Bismol tablets for heartburn, upset stomach, nausea, or indigestion
- Antibacterial cream for cuts, scrapes, blisters, and burns
- Assorted bandages to cover up cuts, scrapes, blisters, and burns
- Hydrocortisone cream for itchy bug bites and rashes
- Tweezers for splinters
- Thermometer

"The last thing to cover is the watch-what-you-eat-the-day-you-travel lesson. So, it was our last day in Siem Reap. We woke up and decided to have breakfast at our hotel, as usual. But this morning, instead of just a plain omelet, I [Pat] decided to make mine a bacon omelet. We had flight reservations to Bangkok out of Siem Reap later that day. At dinner time, I started to think that maybe I didn't feel all that well, but we decided to have dinner anyway. When I got halfway through my meal, I figured that's enough. Carrie became concerned because I never leave anything on my plate (especially when it's a cheeseburger! — ck).

Soon, it was time for the tuk-tuk to take us to the airport. Within 15 minutes of arriving at the airport, I knew that all that food was about to come back up. Miserable, I spent the next two hours running from the waiting area to the bathroom. Fortunately, by the time we boarded, I was completely empty. So, the only thing it could have been was the bacon because otherwise we ate the same things. I have decided not to include pictures of my airport adventure, a gesture which I thought you might appreciate. You'll be relieved to know that, although in the short term I could not even look at bacon, I have regained my love of those delicious strips of pork fat. Lesson learned? Stick with simple, known foods on travel days."

Popping Pink Peptos Like Candy in the Siem Reap, Cambodia, Airport

Flashlight

Even though I almost always have my smartphone with me, which can be used as a flashlight, I still carry a small LED flashlight. It has come in handy many times. If an earring rolls under the bed or I can't locate a small item inside my bag, the little flashlight is easier to use than the phone, and it saves my phone's battery. This particular flashlight has a built-in clip so it can be attached to a strap, zipper-pull, or a ring on a bag, so it's always easy to find.

One time, in Lima, Peru, we nearly had to spend the night outside in the cockpit of our boat. We arrived in the wee hours of the morning and had requested that the yacht club have a lancha (small open motor boat) waiting for us to take us out to our mooring. According to plan, the lancha was there and we were quickly taken to our boat. As the tired-and-ready-to-get-home lancha driver sped away, we immediately found ourselves in a pitch-black cockpit under a moonless sky. We had no flashlight, no cellphone, and couldn't decipher the markings on the combination lock's wheels. Fortunately, I can make an eardrum-shattering whistle. I let out a few high-decibel bursts, and the lancha returned and lent us his light. Having a small flashlight sure would have been useful then!

Sewing Kit

You can buy a kit or make your own. Many times, hotels have free basic sewing kits just for the asking. Hopefully, you won't need to sew often. Things to include if you assemble your own: a few feet of a light-colored thread, a few feet of a dark-colored thread, a needle, a couple of spare buttons, and a couple of safety pins. Cute little scissors aren't necessary as you can always use your nail clippers.

Phone/Wallet Leash

I had my smartphone pickpocketed once, and after replacing it I wanted to make sure that my new phone wouldn't get stolen too. After a quick search, I found a "leash" that I could secure one end of which to my phone's case and the other to my belt. It has a quick-connect fastener making it easy for me to use the phone and then re-secure it when I'm done. To be honest, I don't use it everywhere, but the short section with the ring on it is always attached to my phone. Slipping the ring over my finger eliminates my worries of dropping my phone to the bottom of the ocean or the pavement far below when I'm taking a photo. The leashes are sold in a multi-pack, so Pat uses one on his wallet too.

Games

Cribbage and Farkel are compact and fun games to have. When it's just the two of us and we feel like killing some time, we drag out the travel cribbage board. Playing with actual cards and a scoreboard is far more relaxing than playing a game on a phone or laptop. Besides, we can play together and not be distracted by pop-up email or Facebook notifications. One of these days, I'm going to let Pat win a game or two.

When we're making new friends or there are more than the two of us, we like to play Farkel. Farkel is a dice game with as many variations as there are germs on an amusement park turnstile. It's easy to learn and fun to teach. It also goes remarkably well with wine. We've played it with as few as three people and as many as almost a dozen. It's a great icebreaker, too, in hostel common rooms. The compact version of the game comes in a 35mm film canister, and the unadulterated game rules are written on the outside for easy reference.

> *"After a tough day of sleeping in, drinking coffee, playing Farkel, and walking Cassie, we were all pretty hungry. We made a couple of scrumptious pizzas to enjoy with a bottle or two of Argentine wine. By the way, Roxi's tales of us decimating her nest egg by gambling on Farkel are greatly exaggerated!"*

Farkeling for Fun and Profit in Patagonia

Clothing

Clothing is such a personal thing that it's impossible to tell you what you should pack. Shorts? Dresses? Pants? Kilts? Cold weather? Warm weather? Both? Clothes for fancy restaurants and the theater, or attire for sweaty hikes and a picnic? All of the above?

It's a bit of a balancing act if you plan to be in multiple climates and do both dress-up things and dirty things. The most helpful piece of advice I can give is to plan on layering, and take pieces of clothing that can be mixed and matched ad infinitum.

But don't overpack! Traveling light is the secret to happy travel. Plan on doing laundry once a week while you are on the road. In an emergency, quick-dry clothing can be washed in the bathroom sink by hand with shampoo. Besides, if you do find that you really could have used something you left at home, it's the perfect excuse to go shopping.

The lighter you keep your luggage, the happier you will be on travel days. Articles of clothing that we have found to be ideal for long-term, multi-climate travel include:

- Zip-off Pants: People either love zip-off pants or hate them. I love them and actually pack two pairs. One pair is geared for sweaty, dirty outdoor activities, and the other can pass for business casual when worn as long pants. In Southeast Asia, zip-off pants are great. You can walk around in the humidity and heat in shorts, then zip on the pants to enter a temple, where more modest dress is required. They are also great to have when you start out on a hike in shorts, but then get ambushed by a swarm of mosquitoes.
- Down Jacket: A good down jacket provides a lot of warmth and weighs hardly anything. It also packs compactly, and it will keep you toasty warm in cool weather. For colder weather, add a waterproof breathable rain jacket on top and a thin wool sweater underneath.

"All was status quo until Easter Sunday. We set off on our walk with a pack full of goodies and wine, dressed in our puffy coats (down jackets), trying to fit in. It was a little cooler anyway, so we thought we could bear the added insulation. The puffy coats lasted all of about 15 minutes before we shed and carried them. Soon, we found a well-positioned bench to make our perch for people-watching and then noticed something. The puffy coats and fancy scarves that had been commonplace throughout the entire week were conspicuous by their absence. Where did they go? There were shorts and sandals, bare arms and shoulders, and even a few shirtless boys. What gives?

Was it like not wearing white after Labor Day? Was it inappropriate to wear puffy coats and fancy scarves after Easter? I googled 'Italian puffy coat etiquette' but came up empty. We still don't know why, but the puffy coats that had been ubiquitous were gone."

Contemplating Puffy Coat Etiquette in Genoa, Italy

- Wool/Fleece Sweater: Cashmere sweaters provide excellent warmth without being bulky. They are horrendously expensive, though. Merino wool is also a good choice for a warm, yet thin, sweater and it costs less than cashmere. In addition, both cashmere and merino sweaters look dressy enough for a fine restaurant too. However, if merino wool is still too expensive, you can find thin fleece sweaters that provide decent warmth.
- Mittens and a Hat for Cold Weather: It's easy to forget to pack your hat and mittens if the weather is nice at home.
- Waterproof/Breathable Rain Jacket with Hood: Unless you are spending your entire time in the Sahara Desert, it will probably rain at some point during your trip. Obviously, you want your rain jacket to be waterproof, but you will be more comfortable if it is breathable as well. When you are wrapped up in a non-breathable layer and you exert yourself, you sweat. The water vapor has nowhere to go, and you wind up being just as wet as if you had no rain jacket at all. Also, if your jacket has a hood, you can leave the umbrella at home. And, as mentioned above, a rain jacket also provides another layer of insulation when worn over your sweater and down jacket.
- Microfiber Underwear: Having comfortable, moisture-wicking underwear is of paramount importance. Microfiber underwear is comfortable, takes less room than cotton underwear, and dries in a fraction of the time.

- Polyester Blouses: They are dressy, lightweight, don't wrinkle, dry quickly, and maintain their bright colors.
- Synthetic High-Tech Button-up Shirts: Same idea as the polyester blouses, but they often provide better sun-protection. Some even come with an SPF (Sunscreen Protection Factor) rating.
- Good Walking Shoes: Make sure you love your shoes before you take off. If they can double as your hiking shoes, it will save a lot of room in your bag. Speaking of saving room in your bag, you should wear your biggest shoes/boots on travel days to help lighten your bag. I know it sounds counterintuitive to wear hiking boots through airport security, but it's painless if you untie them and stick the shoelaces inside. It's easy to slip your boots off and stick them through the x-ray machine and then slip them back on when you get to the other side. It's just about as easy as wearing flip-flops.
- Wide-Brimmed Hat: Being fair-skinned, I take sun protection seriously. I spend a lot of time outdoors, and even when wearing sunscreen, my nose and cheeks still burn. The wide-brimmed hat helps mitigate the sun's UV-attack on my face and neck. It's a Tilley hat and is guaranteed for life.

Transportation

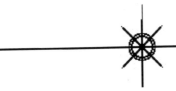

"Getting from Edinburgh to Dublin, I was told, would be a piece of cake. Now, Carrie does a great job of getting us from point A to point B, and since I do none of this planning I can't bitch too much, but in her attempt to be frugal, let me just say that we've had a few adventures. So, you'll understand my skepticism when she said, 'Nah, we're not going to fly to Dublin. We'll take a cab to the bus station, then take a bus across Scotland to catch a ferry to Belfast, then a bus in Belfast to catch another bus to Dublin. And we'll top it off by taking the light rail in Dublin to our Airbnb.' 'Oh, OK, Sounds easy enough. What could possibly go wrong?' I replied with just a hint of sarcasm."

Planning Cost-Effective Transportation from Edinburgh, Scotland, to Dublin, Ireland

Remember when you were a kid and flying was just about the coolest thing in the world? Remember getting off the plane and having friends or family waiting for you right at the gate? Remember leaving your shoes on and keeping your dignity intact when going through security? How did air-travel morph into such an unpleasant experience?

Flying has become my least favorite mode of transportation. I love trains and boats and even prefer taking buses to flying. Sometimes, though, getting from point A to point B in a timely fashion is necessary, or no other way to transit from point A to point B exists, or it is by far the least expensive option. Let's explore how to make the best of flying and discuss other modes of transportation too.

Long-Haul

You've finally decided where to explore, and it's on the other side of the planet. You look at flights and realize that you'll be signing up for 30+ hours in noisy, germ-riddled metal tubes, enduring three or four different airports, and riding in taxis, subways, tuk-tuks, and whatever. Ugh. How on earth do you survive 30+ hours of flights and other transportation to relocate from your home to your first room in the far-flung land you chose to visit?

Flying with an Intermediate City Stop

One way to make a long transit more bearable is to spend a couple of days in an intermediate city. Does the flight go through Taipei? Copenhagen? Reykjavik? Why not spend a few days in Taiwan, Denmark, or Iceland? Jet lag will be less abusive, and you might just find something unexpectedly wonderful in a place that wasn't even on your radar. Hopefully it was on the plane's radar, though.

Sounds good, right? But, how do you actually find multiple legs of one-way airfare without breaking the bank? Isn't the cheapest option to book a roundtrip ticket? Well, sometimes yes and sometimes no. I generally book one-way tickets because, honestly, I have no idea where we are going or how long we'll be staying there. And it seems that most airlines don't try to gouge you as much for a one-way airfare like they used to do.

A halfway-around-the-world trip with an intermediate stop will take some work. Plan to spend a few hours sorting it out. The more flexible you are with dates, the better, and letting the cheap long-haul flight determine your intermediate stop is key. Also, you will want to start finding your airfare no fewer than six weeks before departure. My target cost to fly us from the States to Europe, or from the States to Asia, is no more than $500/person. You can do much better than that if you live in a hub-city.

Step 1: Determine the International Airports Near Your Destination

Say you live in Tucson and want to go to northern Italy. The first thing to do is to make a list of the international airports near your destination that might be suitable. Do a Google search for "international airports in Italy." You'll discover that Genoa, Turin, and Milan are all in the region where you want to start your Italian trip. Don't forget to check adjacent countries too.

Step 2: Eliminate Expensive Airports

Pull up one of the airfare search engines (See Step 3 below for search engines) and plug in your departure city (Tucson), your preferred departure date, and one of the potential arrival cities (Genoa, Turin, Milan). Then run the search and note the lowest price. Don't worry if the lowest-priced route has an awful itinerary. Next, rerun the search for a few different dates on which you could travel. You also want to make sure that a popular local event isn't skewing the results. For example, you do NOT want to fly into Pamplona, Spain, when the Running of the Bulls festival is in full swing. Do this for the other arrival cities you are considering, and use the same dates. In this case, flying into Genoa is consistently more expensive than flying into Turin or Milan, so pick one of those instead.

Step 3: Determine the Long-Haul Carrier

Run your search (Tucson to Milan) through at least three different airfare search engines. The more the merrier. Here are ones I use:

- Cheapflights
- Skyscanner
- Momondo
- Rome2Rio
- Kayak

When I researched the Tucson to Milan example, Momondo and Cheapflights came up with the least expensive airfare at $586/person — above my target of $500 — but the cheapest itineraries were fanny-spanking, 3-stop, longer-than-24hr, agony-machines. I looked at the itineraries for a few of the cheapest routes, though, and noted which airline was doing the long-haul portion. In this case, Norwegian and WOW were frequently used. I asked myself: Where do the flights land, perhaps somewhere I would like to visit? The search returned a Norwegian flight from LAX to Oslo, a WOW flight through Reykjavik, and a Norwegian flight through London. I decided that Oslo looked interesting, so let's use it for our example.

Next, go to the airline's website, in this case Norwegian. Often, airlines offer a low-fare calendar that helps you identify the cheapest day to travel. With the Norwegian website, you can look at the basic fares, called LowFares, for the entire month. You see that the day you prefer to depart has LAX to Oslo fares for $289, but if you leave three days later, the fare is only $199. Or, if you have the flexibility to leave either a week and a half earlier or a week and a half later, the fare is as low as $169. Now don't be super-excited about the fares. You still need to add the cost of baggage, seat assignments, food, and any other add-ons you might want or need.

Most airlines have different levels of service. For Norwegian, the second least expensive fare-type, called LowFare+, includes one checked bag, a seat assignment, and a meal. It's a good choice and runs $259 for the flight that has a LowFare price of $169. You can also add only what you need to the basic fare. Sometimes you can save money by going a la carte, but not on this flight if you need to check a bag and want to choose your seat. A checked bag runs $65 and a reserved seat $45, for $110 total, so it makes more sense to pay the $90 difference between LowFare and LowFare+ for a checked-bag, a seat assignment, and a meal too.

Are you wondering why you might need to check your bag even though it is of carry-on dimensions? Many of the non-US budget airlines have a weight restriction on carry-on bags. With Norwegian, that limit is 10kg for both of your allowed carry-on items combined. Our main bags, although they are of proper carry-on size, weigh in at just under 12kg. Additionally, Pat has a camera bag, kinda hefty, and I carry a plump "purse." The checked bag fee is usually more expensive if you pay it at the airport rather than online when you buy your ticket. You might be able to sneak a heavy bag on board, but we've had our carry-on bags weighed at check-in and had to pay more at the airport. Not fun.

Step 4: Find the First-Leg Transportation

Before booking your long-haul flight, do a sanity check on your first-leg transportation. In this example, you need to go from Tucson to LAX. Run it through one of the airfare search engines, and make sure the price isn't shocking. (Rome2Rio will also give you bus, train, and other options.) If the price seems reasonable, book the long-haul flight before booking anything else. You may also want to do a sanity check on the last-leg too. For what it's worth, I generally book directly with the airline.

Now run your first-leg search through the other search engines. Find the flight that works best for you and book it. In this case, a Delta flight comes up for $81. Further, it doesn't depart at stupid-o'-thirty in the morning, and it still gives ample time to make the connection in LA. Again, I generally book directly with the airline, and checking the Delta website reveals a slightly lower fare of $77. That doesn't include a checked bag, but Delta doesn't have a weight limit, so if your bag is carry-on size, it can fit in the overhead bin. Additionally, Delta lets you pick your seat at no extra charge.

> *"We queued up with the rest of the 'budget travelers' and thought to ourselves, Gee, this line isn't very long. We'll probably have an hour to kill and time to get a much-needed coffee... and pee, of course. After 15 minutes in line, we noticed that we had moved only about two feet, which may have had nothing to do with actual customers being served but rather natural attrition. It started to look like the cup of coffee was unlikely to happen.*

The problem was simple. One Ryan Air agent was single-handedly checking in all of the passengers. Each time a party appeared before him, you'd hear the sigh, the bargaining, and finally the anger, almost like the five stages of grief but in reverse. Some unfortunates were banished to the gigantic line of non-rule-following passengers, while others were permitted to shuffle items from checked bag to carry-on or vice-versa. All left the check-in desk with the same shell-shocked look of people emerging from their first timeshare sales pitch."

The Joys of Flying

Step 5: Find the Final Leg

How long do you want to stay in your intermediate city? Run a search for the date you want to leave Oslo for your destination city, Milan. If your dates are flexible, do what you did with the long-haul flight and find the carriers that run the route. On their website, see if staying an extra day or two results in a better fare. In this case, Ryanair, Brussels Airlines, and Norwegian all offer flights in the $80-$100 range. Only Norwegian has a direct flight, though. Checking the low-fare calendar, you'll see that it pays to stay in Oslo for four nights so that your fare is only $87 (including seat choice and one checked bag).

Is Stopping in an Intermediate City Worth the Effort?

Well, the first-leg costs $77 with you carrying your bag on board. At $259, the long-haul flight to Oslo with a checked bag, seat assignment, and meal is a good deal. Your final-leg flight costs $87 with a checked bag and seat assignment. Happily, you won't have to get up too early since the first flight leaves Tucson at 11:30am and arrives in LA at 1:10pm. That gives you plenty of time to make your connection and even spend a few hours with friends in LA, if you have any, before the 7:40pm transatlantic (transarctic?) flight. You'll arrive in Oslo at 2:55pm the next day, so your mission is to sleep as much as possible on that flight. As an added bonus, you have four days to explore Oslo!

Bottom line: The route comes to $423/person in airfare. That's $163/person better than what the search engines generated because you were flexible with your dates and your intermediate destination. The extra stop also makes getting from Tucson to Milan a much more relaxed experience than the soul-crushing one the search engine cooked up on its own. If that isn't worth a few hours of work, your budget is probably a lot bigger than ours, and you must be one of those rip-the-bandage-off-fast people, a real masochistic money-bags.

Flying - Grin and Bear It

If you don't have time for a stop in an intermediate city, or you just want to get to your final destination as quickly as you can, try to make as few connections as possible. However, give yourself extra time between flights, especially if you're connecting to a different carrier, or if you're arriving internationally and departing domestically. You may need to collect your bags, clear customs and immigration, possibly change terminals, and then recheck your bags. Know before you go how long you should allow for the transfer, and then add an hour or two. Nothing will stress you more than having your first flight delayed and wondering if you'll make your next one.

Another strong suggestion is that you should sleep whenever you can. It is far better to be rested than in sync with the new time zone. People tend to become grumpy and make mistakes when they're tired. Just ask me where my last cell phone went. It's a rare traveler who can actually sleep well on a flight. If you're one of them, I am completely jealous. A sleep mask and earplugs make a world of difference, and they take almost no room in your bag. Neck pillows are popular, and the fleece-covered inflatable ones pack small and are comfortable.

Some people use sleep aids effectively. I tried Ambien... once. My friend took hers with the pre-meal glass of wine, so I did too. Pat was more cautious and took his after the meal. From what I understand, my friend and husband had a good laugh making fun of me while I played with my food. My advice, test drive a sleep aid at home so you know how it will affect you. If you wind up playing with your food on an airplane, the story may still be told 20+ years later.

Also, if you are flying no-frills or low-frills, pack snacks and water. You can take an empty water bottle through security and then fill it up on the other side. Did you know that you can pack alcohol in your carry-on bag? When you go through security, it just needs to be in a 3.4oz (100ml) or less container and presented in a quart-sized zipper bag along with your carry-on liquid/gel toiletries. Some airlines have strict rules about you consuming your own alcohol, so don't do it if that's the case, or at least don't let the flight attendant catch you. That being said, drink alcohol lightly, and drink water frequently while flying. It is easy to become dehydrated, and you don't want to have a headache when you arrive at your destination.

One last note on flying long-haul. Long periods of sitting motionless in cramped quarters can increase your risk of developing deep vein thrombosis (DVT) which means that clots can form in the legs, and they can lead to serious health issues or even death. Stand up and walk around when you aren't sleeping. Lift your heels up and down by doing calf-raises while you're seated. Travelers at risk for DVT include people who are pregnant, obese, undergoing certain cancer treatments, or those who have a family history of DVT. Compression stockings have been shown to reduce the risk of DVT, so if you are at risk, they are cheap insurance. Also, it is believed that staying hydrated can reduce your risk as well. Drink plenty of water and avoid caffeine and alcohol.

Don't Fly - Cruise!
Flying isn't the only way to travel overseas. In fact, the key word is "sea." A friend turned us on to repositioning cruises. A repositioning cruise is just what you would think it is. When the cruising season changes from one area to another, the cruise lines reposition their ships to an area of higher demand. You can find transatlantic and transpacific itineraries as well as ones that voyage up and down the east and west coasts of the States. Repositioning cruises even go to and from South America. Keep in mind, though, they are available only at certain times of the year and only in one direction at that time.

Repositioning cruises can also be amazingly affordable. Our friend recommended that we use VacationsToGo to search for cheap cruises. The website is easy to use and full of great deals. On the website, under Find A Bargain, change All Cruise Regions to Repositioning, then click Show Me The Deals. As I look at my screen now, I see one that goes from Ft. Lauderdale to Rome in 14 days for $499 per person based on double occupancy. (Note: The prices go down the closer the departure date, but you run the risk of the cruise selling out.) Taxes, fees, and port expenses are not included in that number and neither is the gratuity. On this particular cruise, the taxes, fees, and port expenses are $126/person, and the gratuity is automatically charged to your onboard account at $12.50/day/passenger. That works out to about $114/day for two people before extras (internet, booze, anything spent on shore). It's a little above our $100/day budget, but remember, that figure is merely an average. The over-budget amount can be cleared by pet sitting for a week, finding really inexpensive lodging, doing inexpensive activities, and/or cooking for yourself.

Start checking for deals about three months ahead of time, and check back frequently. I nailed the bargain-basement price of $449/person on our 13-day cruise just ten weeks before the sailing date. The price actually went up after that, and the cruise eventually sold out.

Following our friend's recommendation, we had to give a repositioning cruise a try, so we took the Norwegian Epic from Barcelona to Port Canaveral, Florida, in early November 2017. As our friend suggested, we booked the cruise through VacationsToGo. Making the reservation, getting questions answered, and paying were all easy. Be sure to check the rates directly with the cruise line too. Sometimes they offer perks (free upgrade to a cabin with a balcony, a drink package, onboard credit, etc.) that aren't passed on to the cruise brokers.

It was our first cruise ever, so we were curious to see if we would like it. Some people love cruising and others not so much. If you have never cruised, here is what we learned:

Check-in and Embarkation

This was unfortunately not much different than the check-in and screening process at an airport. A window of time was given during which to check in, and we were instructed not to arrive at the pier more than an hour before that window. That's what they said anyway. When we arrived at the pier in Barcelona at the earliest time suggested, the line was already quite long. It seemed that the professional cruisers (PCs) knew to come early.

Once at the pier, we presented our cruise documents to the baggage person, who tagged our main bags with our cabin number and tossed them onto a cart. I assume that bag-checkers ran the bags through an x-ray machine, but surprisingly the bag-checkers, if they existed, allowed our liter of scotch in a plastic bladder to pass through. Keep in mind that you will be separated from your bag for a few hours, so take anything you need with you. PCs took their swimsuits with them and smiled at us smugly from the hot tubs and pools which they had all to themselves.

After we were separated from our main bags, we queued up with the thousands, literally, of other people trying to board the ship. The port security officials ran us through a metal detector and our carry-on bags through an x-ray machine. The good news is that the TSA wasn't running the show, and there were none of those full-body x-ray machines that illuminate your naughty bits for others to see.

Next, we joined another line to check-in, set up our onboard account, and receive our cabin keys. On our cruise, the cabin keys were cards. They served not only as our keys, but also as our Cruiser ID and as our onboard credit card. Don't lose your card! It's like cash. PCs had straps around their necks and somehow had put holes in their cards to attach them to the straps.

At this point in the process, we thought we were done. Not so fast. Next, we hiked up the ramp and finally boarded the ship. We had to hand over our bottles of wine to a ship's official so they could be sequestered until the day before the cruise ended. The policies on how many bottles you may bring on board vary from cruise line to cruise line. Norwegian permitted us two bottles of wine (not liquor), which were marked with our name and then inventoried. We were then issued a receipt so that we could retrieve them later. On Norwegian, you can request your bottle at any time, but you will be charged a steep corkage fee if you do. If you wait until the day before the cruise ends, though, you pay no corkage fee and you are free to drink your wine to your heart's content.

But wait! There's more! Now we had to go through yet another metal detector and our carry-on bags through another x-ray machine. After this last screening, we were done. Finally, we were free to go to the buffet, hang out on deck, and explore the ship while waiting for the announcement that the cabins were ready. The whole embarkation process took about two hours.

The Cabin

If you booked the cheapest cabin, like we did, and didn't score an upgrade, like we didn't, your cabin is what is called an "inside cabin." What that means is that you don't have a window or a balcony. I'm sure it would have been enjoyable to have had a window or a balcony with its view of the sea, but as it turned out, we didn't spend much time in the room anyway. The cost-to-benefit ratio didn't make it worth the additional cost to upgrade our cabin. In fact, the ship had many common areas, on-deck and inside, where we could relax and enjoy the view, and lots of activities to keep us entertained.

The inside cabin on the Norwegian Epic was remarkably comfortable and did not feel cramped at all. The closet was large and easily held all of our belongings. The shower was bigger than many of the ones we had while in Europe and the two of us could fit in it, but that's probably too much information. The bed was queen-sized and we slept well on it. The TV had few channels, but we liked to put on the "Bridge View" or the "Cruise Data" channel. The "Bridge View" channel served as our window as it broadcast a view from the ship's bridge, which its name clearly indicates. We'd turn the sound off and leave it on all night so that we could tell when it was daylight, which arrived an hour later every two days.

The cabin came with a cabin steward. He was our dedicated housekeeper, mailman (daily newsletters and ship correspondence), ice-getter, and more. He was also fond of making animal sculptures out of our towels and was particularly adept at making monkeys. Although a gratuity was automatically charged to our account each day, we learned from PCs that it is customary to leave your cabin steward an additional gift at the end of the cruise.

Dining

Norwegian Cruise Lines had what they called "Freestyle Cruising." They did not assign a dining time or a table as we understand they do on other cruise lines. Instead, there were several restaurants to choose from, and we could eat at whatever time we liked. We could also choose to sit with others or by ourselves. As you'd imagine, the ship had dressy restaurants, casual restaurants, and, of course, the buffet, the most informal of all. Food was available 24/7.

In addition to the restaurants included in the fare, the Epic had specialty restaurants for an additional charge. Obviously, we didn't try any because of our budget-consciousness, but also because the included restaurants and the buffet had excellent food. Did I mention the ubiquitous ice cream machines? It was a good thing the ship had a gym because overeating was extremely easy to do!

Drinking

Cruise ships in general have several bars, and the Epic was no slouch in that regard. Each bar had a different theme, and a theme to suit anyone's taste. Pat is a huge Beatles fan, and he was delighted that one of the bars was fashioned after The Cavern Club where the Beatles rose to fame. Cover bands played Beatles' tunes and the stage was a mock-up of the original. Another generality about cruise ships is that the drinks are expensive. As you well know, we enjoy a tipple, or two, or sometimes three, but drinking on a cruise ship is not budget-friendly. To cut costs, you have four choices: 1.) Luck out and find a cruise with a drink-package included in the fare. 2.) Abstain (I crack myself up). 3.) Smuggle your whistle-wetter of choice on board. 4.) Drink only in port (but not necessarily only Port). We didn't luck out with an included drink-package, and we didn't abstain...

Although the drinks in the bars were pricey, and we weren't allowed to bring our own, occasionally they were free. Yes, free. Well, how do you get in on that action? To discover where and when the complimentary cocktails are available, check the activities in the daily newsletter. Also, be sure to cruise by the duty-free store and look for signs promoting special tasting events. For example, on the Epic, art auctions happened almost every day, and to encourage lively bidding, these events inevitably involved wine and cheese. The duty-free store also hosted a Johnny Walker scotch-tasting event. The representatives giving the presentation wanted to sell expensive bottles, so they showed us an engaging film and then let the fancy scotch flow. I saw a couple of bottles of Johnny Blue purchased by some well-lubricated tasters.

> *The atmosphere aboard was fairly relaxed. There were no dress codes (although clothes were required), we were free to eat at any time at a variety of different restaurants, and there were many planned activities to keep the masses entertained. We only availed ourselves of one activity, however, a Johnny Walker scotch tasting. It was fun, with the host's intent of getting us a bit blitzed so that we could more easily reach into our wallets in order to purchase their $200 bottles. However, as anyone who has read our blogs knows, we are drinking pros. The pours were heavy and we smiled and nodded as we drank their top shelf expensive whiskies, before waddling back to our cabin, wallet still well secured in its pocket.*

Sipping Fine Scotch for Free on a Cruise Ship

The Infirmary
Well, shit happens... so to speak, and so does vomit. Pat must have picked up something bad in Barcelona and wound up violently ill only two nights into our cruise. He had a fever and couldn't keep a thing in him. None of the other passengers on board were ill, nor was I.

The following morning, I called the infirmary early and explained his symptoms. The person who took the call told me that the infirmary wasn't open yet, but they could call the doctor and charge us a butt-load of money for an off-hours consultation. I was also instructed to keep Pat under quarantine and confined to his quarters, except for making his way to the infirmary.

When opening hours at the infirmary finally arrived, and Pat was no better, we went to see the doctor. He drew blood, administered antibiotics, gave him IV fluids and a fever reducer, then kept him for four hours before he released the patient back to the cabin under quarantine. The infirmary was a lifesaver, and Pat was back on his feet in a day. His resurrection did not come inexpensively, though. The bill was a nauseating $1,800! That's 18 days of our budget and a prime example of why travel insurance or international health insurance is so important.

Ports of Call

Our repositioning cruise stopped in only two ports on our way to Florida. After having traveled slowly through Europe, we were shocked to have only six to eight hours to see a place. Pat was quarantined for our first port of call, so it was refreshing to be off the ship in the Azores. However, with such little time there, we couldn't even scratch the surface of what the Azores had to offer.

Shore excursions were available that would take us to the highlights, but they were expensive and not our thing. When we disembarked, local guides and taxi drivers swarmed the dock to hawk their own tours. Bypassing these options, we picked up a free map at the tourist information booth and located a nearby park. Along the way we stopped at a small grocery store and bought some snacks and a couple of beers for lunch. It was a beautiful park and a pleasant change to sit under the trees and listen to nature... and watch the people on the shore excursion be herded quickly by.

Entertainment

The cruise ship was full of entertainment options. Gamblers could gamble at tables or machines. Sun-worshippers could worship El Sol. Party-animals could dance the night away. Spa-dwellers could marinate in the spas. Live shows and music were performed day and night. Pools, hot tubs, and water slides abounded. If bowling was your thing, the Epic even had a bowling alley.

Our favorite activities were a little less structured. After breakfast, we'd head to the gym to burn some calories so we could eat something decadent later. We also liked to go to the Bridge Viewing Room a couple of times a day to check the ship's position, course, and speed, and to ascertain other pertinent sea-going information. After that excitement, we'd sometimes adjourn to one of the nightclubs that was designated as a quiet area until 2pm, where we'd read or write until we were hungry for lunch. Sometimes, too, we'd spend time walking the decks getting exercise and people-watching. In the afternoons, we'd break down and have a crazy-expensive beer on the aft-deck and stare out to sea.

Shopping and Other Ways to Part with Your Money
For many people, shopping is entertainment. I, on the other hand, am a Timex Ironman-wearing, SuperCuts-coiffed, unscented, plain clothes-wearing sort of person. I loathe shopping and so was peeved that the shopping alley always seemed to be located between us and food. It was clearly intentional.

First, we'd pass the Watch Island that always had "One-day specials you absolutely must see!" and a drawing they'd want us to enter. Then we'd try to avoid being spritzed by the perfuminators. The walk past the high-end clothing and accessories boutiques was fairly easy, and we actually window-shopped a little at the duty-free store. The last phase of the budgetary assault was for this "handsome couple" to sneak by the bored and lonely photographer with the cheesy backdrops. What was the thought-process behind the mountain-meadow-with-butterflies backdrop? Come on. This was a monstrous ship in the middle of an ocean, not the hills around Salzburg!

Even our path to the gym had monetary landmines. Women in spa uniforms threatened to massage or exfoliate us if we didn't hurry past them and into the gym. And even there, that holy of holies, was a place to unload both flab and funds. The front desk at the gym had a cheerful person who wished us a good morning and then asked if we wanted to join a for-fee class. I also stopped being kind to another front desk guy after he looked at my belly and asked if I wanted to join the abs class.

Disembarkation

Our disembarkation experience went surprisingly well. We had the option of carrying our own bags off the ship or having them taken down by the crew to be retrieved at a baggage claim. The shuttle service we had arranged to take us from the port into Orlando highly recommended the first option, and I'm glad that we took their advice. A passenger we had met on board in one of the dining rooms emailed us that evening and relayed the alarming news that it had taken him six hours to disembark and transfer to his hotel in Orlando. It took us a mere two hours, and one hour of that was spent on the shuttle between the port and Orlando. Our dinner companion had made the egregious mistake of opting to retrieve his bags from baggage claim.

What We Learned

Most importantly, we learned that we are in the 'not so much' category when it comes to cruising, but we'd do it again if we could replace a long-haul flight. It was cost-effective, and it was a good time to reflect on the eight months we'd been bopping around Europe.

Short-Haul

After sea-faring or sky-faring, once you have reached the continent of your choosing, you still need to travel from city to city. Now, you have many more options than just a plane or boat. Trains, buses, ferries, and more fill the rails, roads, and waterways. This is where Rome2Rio and GoEuro (in Europe) really shine because in addition to finding cheap flights, they pull up other modes of transportation too.

Plane

With the rise of the budget carrier, flying is often the cheapest method of travel. It still comes with all of the drawbacks of flying: security screenings, restrictions on what you may and may not carry on, cramped seating, little booger-eaters kicking the back of your seat, etc., but intracontinental flights can knock many hours off your transit time and add them to your exploration time.

To find the cheap fares, use the same airfare search engines that I mentioned earlier in the Long-Haul section of this chapter. Here are the search engines again for your convenience:

- Cheapflights
- Skyscanner
- Momondo
- Rome2Rio
- Kayak

Run a search for the date you want to fly. If your dates are flexible, do as you did in the long-haul flight example. Find the carriers that run the route, go to their website, and see if waiting an extra day or two results in a better fare. If you are considering other options like train, bus, or ferry, check Rome2Rio and GoEuro (in Europe) too.

Note that on departing a country by air, some countries charge a departure tax. More often than not this fee is included in the price of your airline ticket, but at other times you must pay with cash at the airport or a designated bank. Rarely are departure taxes imposed when you leave a country by land, and when they are, they are generally small. Be sure to reserve the proper amount of cash for the departure tax if one applies. Check your guidebook or search online to see if your travel plans will incur such a fee.

Train
Trains are often an economical way to travel, and traveling by train is infinitely more relaxing than flying. Is your bag larger than a carry-on? Relax. Do you have a few bottles of wine with you? Relax. Are you six-foot-six and concerned about leg-room? Relax. It is difficult to speak generally about trains, though, because riding the rails differs greatly from country to country. Still, commonalities do exist and they are

what make train travel so much more enjoyable than air travel.

First of all, baggage can be of any size and weight as long as you can move it on and off the train in a timely fashion. You are even allowed to carry more than two bags. Some trains have overhead racks for your luggage, others have blocks of shelves, but some, commuter trains in particular, don't have a spot for your bags other than your lap and under your seat. Fortunately, commuter trains are generally used for short distances, usually journeys that last no longer than an hour or so. It is always best to travel light, but that's not mandatory on a train.

A further benefit is that security screenings are non-existent and you can arrive at the train station thirty minutes before your departure instead of hours before a flight. Nine-ounce tubes of toothpaste, knives, bottles of booze, and other airline contraband don't raise an eyebrow in a train station. You can keep your shoes on, leave your laptop in your bag, and avoid an unwanted dose of radiation. So many plusses.

Most importantly, trains are comfortable! Take your seat and enjoy some leg- and elbow-room. Stare out the large windows and observe the countryside. No need to "fasten your seatbelt." In fact, I can't recall ever seeing a seatbelt on a train and definitely never a fasten-seatbelt light. As I remarked, legroom is generous, but if you need to stretch a little more, stand up and walk around. Pay a visit to the dining car or bar car, if the train has one.

Logistically, however, it is important to know a few things about train travel:

Be sure to buy your ticket well in advance of your departure time. If you intend on purchasing your ticket at the station, give yourself extra time. Sometimes ticket machines act up, and lines at ticket windows can be long. Your best bet, if it is possible in your situation, is to purchase your ticket online or at the station days in advance. If different classes are offered, know what you are getting. Some trains have 1st, 2nd, and 3rd class seating. While 1st class cars may have air-conditioning and comfy-seats, 2nd class ones may have comfy-seats but no air-conditioning, and 3rd class may have hard bench seats and no air-conditioning. Overnight trains have different types of sleeping arrangements, and the cars can be air-conditioned or not. Choose the right class for your budget and comfort.

When you arrive at the train station, determine from which platform your train will depart. Go to the platform at least 15 minutes before departure because occasionally you can find signs that indicate the order of the cars in the train. (Your car number and seat number, if you have a reserved seat, will be on your ticket.) If you don't find a sign, you can usually find a railway official walking the platform who is happy to answer questions. Try to ascertain approximately where to be on the platform so you enter the correct car. It's not a problem if you don't enter the correct car, but you will need to maneuver your bags down the aisles and through the doors between cars until you find your seat if you happen to pick the wrong car. Also, some trains make very brief stops. Don't take too much time trying to figure it out on the platform. Get on the train!

"It was go-into-Florence-and-explore day. We've learned that driving in rural areas or on highways is fine, however, neither the Google B*tch nor I are no match for the octopi city roads or the speed-demon Italian drivers. So, Carrie found a small town about halfway between Diacetto and Florence with a small train station. It provided convenient entry into the village and also had easy access to free parking. Everyone was safer because I didn't have to drive into Florence. Eager to get under way, we were off at the crack of dawn, and all went as planned. Exploring Florence made for a lovely day, but now it was time to head home. We were getting a later start back home than we had anticipated, but no problem, the 20-minute train ride would have us back to our waiting chariot by around 10pm.

When we arrived at the station, we were pleased to see that the train was already waiting at platform 16 and was ready for boarding. There was a train attendant at the end car, and we asked him if this was indeed our train. He nodded and motioned us to board the end car.

Twenty minutes later we pulled into our small train station, but, in a panic-inducing moment, we were unable to get the door to open. Through the darkness, we could see that there was no platform for us to exit onto. Sh*t! The train was longer than the station platform, and we were in the rear car. We ran forward, but too late, so the train departed for Pontassieve with us still on it.

Fortunately, we found two off-duty policemen heading home, explained our dilemma, and asked if they could suggest a solution. They tried to be helpful, but alas, they had no definitive solution. 'Maybe you can find a taxi to take back to Sieci,' one suggested. 'At this hour?' the other cop bemoaned. We exited the train at Pontassieve a bit panicked, but a young man came up to us, told us that he had overheard our plight and offered to help. There was a train on the next platform, so he ran to find a conductor with us close behind him and asked if the train stopped at Sieci. 'Yes, it does,' replied the conductor. 'Get on, hurry!' shouted the young man. With barely enough time to say grazie, we were off. Fifteen minutes later we were in the chariot and home by 11pm. Nice to know that kind people still exist."

How Not to Exit a Train - Florence, Italy

Getting off the train can present a few challenges. In countries with punctual train service, you can rely on the expected arrival time to know when you should gather your bags and move toward the doors. In other countries, relying on the arrival time stamped on your ticket may not produce the best results. If you have a phone with a data plan, follow your progress using Google Maps. Google Maps has train stations and routes in its database, so it is easy to see where the stations are and how close you are to them. If you don't have mobile data, have a copy of the route with you, or look for one posted on the wall or bulkhead. Note the name of the station before yours, then pay close attention to the station names. An alternate suggestion, one that we have used successfully, is to ask the conductor to alert you when it is nearly time to alight.

An outstanding resource for all-things-train is The Man in Seat Sixty-One. There's absolutely nothing I could tell you about train travel that isn't thoroughly covered on The Man in Seat Sixty-One's excellent website. The writer covers train travel world-wide. Rome2Rio does a good job of finding train schedules, but The Man in Seat Sixty-One has detailed information about the different train classes and sleeping cars, including photos, schedules, and information on how to buy your ticket.

> *"With the evening sustenance activities complete and 10pm quickly approaching, it was time to turn in for the night. The arrangement was comfortable. There were two bunk beds. We sat on the lower beds while socializing, but for sleeping the girls took the uppers and the boys took the lowers. The door could be locked from the inside, and there was ample room for our bags. The mattresses were firm, but I slept well enough and think the others did too.*
>
> *Very early the next morning the PA system came alive with a sound much like that of a cat trying to climb out of a meat grinder. The 'music' continued for a good 10 minutes, and then an unintelligible announcement was made. At least it was a human voice and the cat was out of its misery. About five minutes after that we arrived at a station. By our estimates, our stop, Hue, Vietnam, was two more cat wailings down the line. As expected, the cat-grinding occurred a couple more times, and then eventually the train arrived at our station."*

The Overnight Train from Hanoi to Hue, Vietnam

Ferry

Ferries come in many shapes and sizes and cross anything from a stream, to a lake, to a sea. Some are as simple as a bamboo raft pulled by hand along a rope strung between two trees, while others are practically cruise ships. If you are in a watery part of the world, and despise flying as much as we do, consider taking a ferry.

For a general idea of where the major ferries run to and from, take a look at Google Maps. Plug in Athens, Greece, for example. You'll notice dotted blue lines emanating from Piraeus, a port city just a short distance from Athens. Those dotted blue lines are the ferry routes. The more you zoom in, the more detail you get. In fact, some of the minor routes won't show up until you zoom in a bit.

Google Maps is helpful in locating ports, but to find ferry lines, schedules, and rates, Direct Ferries is the resource you need. Direct Ferries searches all of the ferry lines, and then shows you the lowest fares and sailing times. One thing I don't like about Direct Ferries is that it doesn't provide passenger reviews. If your search returns three different ferry lines all at about the same price, how do you know if one line is better than the others without reviews? Here is what you do. Go to TripAdvisor, click on the magnifying glass search icon, and type in the name of the ferry line for which you want reviews. Now you have reviews!

Once you select the ferry you wish to take, you choose the type of seat or cabin that you want and then you'll be shown the revised fare. The price won't change if you select the lowest class available, but if you want an upgrade, it will cost a bit more. The website is a little clunky in that it doesn't show you a list of the fares for all available seat-types and cabin-types. You need to select one at a time and click "update." Even though it's cumbersome to view the pricing, Direct Ferries makes it easy and convenient to buy a ticket online.

If you are taking a daytime ferry, the lowest class seat will be just fine. Ferries generally have decent seats and numerous lounges. Arrive at the pier early, though, because the seats are not assigned.

If you are taking an overnight ferry, you can elect to sleep in a regular seat, or you can sometimes upgrade to a reserved seat that's more comfortable and reclines farther, or you can even upgrade to a cabin. If you are a couple traveling together, a cabin may fit into your budget. Since you are traveling overnight, the fare not only includes your transportation, but also your accommodation. Often, the cost-to-comfort ratio is worthwhile and not a budget-breaker. By booking a cabin, you have not only a place in which to escape the crowds and enjoy some quiet, but most importantly a place where you can get a good night's sleep in a real bed and so be well-rested when you arrive at your destination. Additionally, you can lock your bags in the cabin and enjoy prowling the decks and lounges unencumbered.

Ferries often have restaurants and bars as well. The food is of varying quality and prices can be inflated. Your best bet is to pack your own food and drink, especially if you are bumping up against your daily budget.

> *"So, why did we decide to visit Albania? Well, why not? The Lonely Planet described Tirana, the capital, as 'loud, crazy, colorful, and dusty' with 'traffic likened to unmitigated chaos.' Sounds charming, no?*
>
> *We boarded a ferry in Bari, Italy, to cross the Adriatic to Durrës, Albania, which lies just west of the capital city of Tirana. It was an overnight passage, so we had plenty of time to cast about suspicions of what we might find and form a mental image of the former communist country. Hmmm... 'dusty' with 'chaotic traffic.' Sounded a lot like India or parts of Central America. Were we going to have hot showers? Potable water? Please, no, not squatty toilets."*

Our First Overnight Ferry - Italy to Albania

Bus

If you are not in a watery part of the world where a ferry is available, a bus may serve your needs. Buses don't conjure up the romantic visions that trains do, or even ferries for that matter, but it's possible to find some rather comfortable ones. The budget appreciates them too as they are usually the least expensive option. Rome2Rio is a good source for finding routes, bus lines, and approximate fares. If the bus line has a website, Rome2Rio will provide the link and often you can purchase your tickets online.

In Central and South America, it is common for buses to have different classes of seats: regular, semi-cama, and cama. "Cama" means "bed" in Spanish, so if you are taking an overnight bus or a nearly-double-digit-hour-long ride, spring for the highest class of seat you can afford. Once, we were on a nearly 20-hour ride from Mendoza to Bariloche, Argentina, and opted for the "cama" seats. They didn't recline to flat, but they were comfortable enough to afford us some sleep.

Also, in Central and South America, it is not unusual to be served a boxed meal on long rides. Check your ticket because if no meal is included, it may be a long time before you can get off the bus to buy bus station food, and it's never everything you'd hoped it would be. I can't recall if it was in Chile or Argentina, but on one bus we were served wine, a meal, and a post-meal whisky!

In light of that, let's not forget the "chicken-buses." They are neither comfortable nor reliable. Their only saving grace is that they are dirt-cheap. In Central America, old US school buses are pressed into service as public transportation and it's common to see some interesting carry-on items, chickens being one of them.

In Southeast Asia, minibuses are popular. Once again, Rome2Rio can help you find the routes, bus lines, and approximate fares. You can also ask the staff at your guesthouse for help. They are usually able and happy to arrange your transportation.

> *"To get to Phosavanh from Vang Vieng requires a 6-hour minibus ride through narrow and extremely rough mountain roads with an untold number of hairpin turns. Add in the fact that the minibus, with an old and abused suspension, is packed with 11 passengers plus luggage, and the result is an extremely unpleasant experience. Unbelievably, only one dog on the road was killed during the drive. However, many pigs, chickens, and children nearly met the same fate."*

A White-Knuckled Minibus Ride in Laos

In Europe, FlixBus is a reliable bus line with new buses offering free Wi-Fi, a bathroom, and decent leg-room. It's best to pack snacks and water, though, because you never know if you'll have an opportunity to leave the bus, and boxed lunches are not included. On some routes, you are given 15 minutes or so at each major station, and sometimes even half an hour or more, but at other times you are granted no time at all.

On a long bus ride, or train ride for that matter, you will be asleep at some point. Guard your valuables. Do not put anything you can't lose in the overhead bin or under the seat. The safest option is to put your important documents and electronics into a bag you can wear. Put the bag in your lap with the strap around your neck, and then wrap yourself, and it, in a blanket or your jacket. You will sleep better, and thieves will see you as too risky a target.

> *"There was some excitement on the bus around 3am when a woman from Germany whom we had met prior to boarding the bus realized that she had been robbed. There was much shouting, and eventually the police were called and boarded the bus. Initially, they did not find the money that was stolen, but a second search after the bus pulled into the terminal resulted in the money being retrieved. Turns out it was one of the bus employees. Apparently, they didn't search the employees' bags during the first pass. Just goes to show that you can never let your guard down."*

Overnight Bus from Santiago to Valdivia, Chile

Another note on protecting valuables on a bus: High-tech or new-looking backpacks or suitcases are prime targets. We heard more than a few stories of people having their entire backpack stolen from the hold on a bus. If you are using a new backpack or a fancy suitcase, also take a really cheap, crappy-looking, nylon duffle bag into which you can stuff your luggage. The crappier the duffle bag looks, the better.

Ridesharing
This is where Rome2Rio does an admirable job. One time, we were in Granada, Spain, and wanted to take a bus to Seville, but all of the cheap buses at a reasonable time of

day were full. A search on Rome2Rio saved our bacon. In addition to bus, train, plane, and rental car options, an option came up for "Rideshare" with a range of decent rates. That is how we discovered BlaBlaCar, the internet-enabled hitchhiking service.

> *"We had no idea what type of car we would be riding in, nor anything about our driver. We were his first passengers, and he was our first BlaBlaCar driver. A few minutes after the designated pickup time, a beautiful BMW pulled up in front of us and our driver emerged. He spoke no English, so we put our best Spanish speaker, Carrie, in the front seat. Long story short, it was a fun 2.5-hour journey during which we interacted as well as we could with our driver who was very kind and patient. We'll definitely give BlaBlaCar another shot when it fits our travel needs."*

Hitchhiking Via the Internet for the First Time - Granada to Seville, Spain

Unfortunately, BlaBlaCar isn't available in the United States or Canada. It's a French company, and most of the service it offers is in Europe, including parts of Eastern Europe. BlaBlaCar is not a taxi service for short rides, like Uber or Lyft. The focus of the service is to match riders with unused seats in cars traveling long distances.

When you search for a BlaBlaCar ride, you can read reviews about the driver. It is important to make sure the driver has at least a few good reviews and no bad ones. Also check how much luggage you are allowed. Some of those European cars are pretty tiny, and the driver might have a friend or spouse traveling with them, and they have luggage too. One way to ensure that your luggage will fit is to buy all three back seats. You can always put your bags on the seat.

When you create your BlaBlaCar account, you provide a payment method: credit card, PayPal, etc. No cash ever exchanges hands. When the ride is over, you receive a message asking if your ride was successful. You say yes, and then the driver is paid. You don't need to have a voice/text-capable phone to use BlaBlaCar, but it does help.

That way, if your driver is running late, he or she can let you know.

Having conversations with the drivers is always interesting and fun and using BlaBlaCar is also a wonderful way to not only see the country from a local's perspective but to gain information about your destination. One couple who drove us from Florence, Italy, to Rome were a real hoot. He was Roman and she was Neapolitan. Upon learning that we intended to visit Naples as well as Rome, they launched into a bidding war, basically, with stories of why their beloved city was superior to the other. It was all in fun and the hours spent in the car flew by. As an added bonus, in most countries, the fare is about the same as a fare for a bus. Not so in France, unfortunately. I think it has to do with the expensive toll roads.

Local Transit

Congratulations! You have made it to the city you were aiming for and... it's big. It's Really BIG. You could never walk to all of the places that you'd like to see in the time you have allotted. How do you move about now?

Public Transportation

Metros, trams, trolleys, buses, even water taxis, can be found in nearly every major metropolitan area in the world. For a typical city-dweller, they are a familiar and an obvious way to move about inexpensively. For the inexperienced non-city-dweller, they can be intimidating and a bit confusing to the point where it would be better not to mess with them and to opt for a more expensive taxi or shuttle service. Fear not!

While they are all different, they are similar in quite a few ways. Remember, public transport systems are meant for the public, not just theoretical physicists. You can do this! Here are a few bits of information that will make you love these low-cost people-movers.

How to Get from Point A to Point B
A.k.a. Where are the stops/stations, and when should I be there? Well, it's Google Maps to the rescue yet again. Most

of the major cities have their public transportation schedules available on Google Maps. Just plug in your destination, click Directions, and then click the little icon that looks like a tram. You can use the schedule explorer to search for times in the future too. Great. Now you have the number of the bus or the name of the metro/tram/trolley line, the location of the departure stop or station, a departure time, the name of the direction, and the name of your final stop. Google Maps even provides the walking directions for the sections you need to do on foot.

> *"Following the directions provided by Google Maps, we jumped onto the metro and like pros made a change and then got off at the correct station. The Google B*tch routed us through the back-ends of commercial buildings. Thankfully some guys were at one of the loading docks and, as if they'd seen people wandering around lost before, they asked in English, 'Museum?' We nodded. In unison they pointed at a gap in the fence toward a hinky set of rusty metal stairs. We cautiously made our way down the tetanus-fraught gauntlet of rusty metal, and like magic, the ugly, communist-era, square cement building with absolutely no character appeared. We knew it was the right place because at least half a dozen Lenin statues and a giant red star graced the lawn."*

Using Google Maps for Public Transportation and Walking Directions in Sofia, Bulgaria

If Google Maps doesn't have the public transportation schedules, you can usually acquire a map and schedule at a tourist information center or find any station or stop and look for a map and schedule plastered on the wall. On the map, find the name of the stop where you plan to board the public transportation, probably right where you're standing and marked with "You are here." Run your finger along the route that goes to your destination. Note the bus number or tram/trolley/metro line and the name of the stop where you want to go. Now, run your finger all the way to the end of the route, past your stop, and note that stop's name too. That's the terminus and also the direction of your bus/tram/trolley/metro. It will be displayed on the platforms or on a sign on the bus.

It is vital to note the direction. If you are not going all the way to the end of the line, it will be a different name than your stop. The direction might be obvious when you're using above-ground transport, but once you descend into the underground labyrinth of the subway, it's easy to become disoriented.

It doesn't matter if you use Google Maps, a paper map, or if you obtain directions from a person, here are the important pieces of information that you need to know:

- The bus number or Tram/Trolley/Metro line name
- The name and location of the departure stop/station
- The departure time or departure frequency (last return is good to know too)
- The name of the terminus (last stop) that's the direction you're going
- The name of your destination stop

Ok, you're on the public transportation. How do you know when to get off? Good question! Most modes of transportation have a map of the route posted and a scrolling sign indicating the next stop or sometimes illuminating dots right on the map. On metros, subways, and trams, the vehicle will stop at each station. Make a mental note of the station name before your stop so you know when to move toward the doors.

Buses don't necessarily stop at every bus stop, and you may not be able to read the names of the stops if the bus whizzes right by them. Knowing approximately what time you should arrive and a few cross-streets or landmarks is helpful, but the easiest way to know when your stop is near is to follow your progress on Google Maps. Enter your starting point and destination, and then request the public transportation directions (click the tram icon). Now you can see how close you're getting to your destination. Another note about riding public buses is that you often need to indicate that you wish to be let off at the next stop by pushing a button. Watch the locals and do what they do.

Buying and Using a Ticket

Most subway/metro systems have ticket kiosks that can be operated in English and take either credit cards or cash. Many also have ticket windows with an actual human being, which is helpful if you're unsure about your route or if the machines are acting up.

Buying a bus ticket can be done in many different ways, but it is probably best to ask a local ahead of time, or someone at the bus stop, how to purchase a ticket. Email your host, for example. The most common way is to pay the driver directly, and they always appreciate exact change if you have it. In Central America, it is usual to take a seat, then a "helper" comes and collects your money. In Italy, tickets need to be purchased at Tabacs/Newsstands. Watch what other people do, and don't be afraid to ask a stranger for help. You will find more often than not that people are happy to assist you. It sounds like a hassle, but you only need to figure it out once, and when you do you are on your way to being a bus-riding pro.

> *"Actually, we got off to a rather bad start in Turin. We needed to catch a local bus to get us to our Airbnb, but we were told that you had to buy the tickets at a Tabac shop, all of which were closed. Long story short, we hopped on a trolley without tickets, rode it to within 1km of our lodging, got off and hiked the rest of the way. It's a really terrible way to run a transportation system. Everywhere else that we've gone you could buy tickets on the bus, but not in Turin."*

Learning to Have a Few Spare Tickets On-hand in Turin, Italy

Whew! That sounded harder than it really is, but now you have your ticket. Many times, you need to validate your ticket. Seriously? This is sounding complicated. Relax. You only need to figure this out once, too, and then you'll know for the next time. Metros and subways are easy. If you need to insert your ticket into a turnstile to enter a platform, that is your validation. For other modes of transportation, validation machines might be right on the bus/tram/trolley or at the stop/platform. They are little machines into which you feed your ticket, and they stamp the date and time on your ticket, sometimes in ink, sometimes electronically. Always assume you will need to validate your ticket until you find out differently. Look for signs, ask an official-looking person, ask other riders. Don't skip this step because random ticket-checks do occur, and the penalty can be a big hit to the budget.

Transfers

You've searched for your directions and Google Maps has given you a route, but the route includes a transfer. Oh, no! Hold on. Transfers aren't the end of the world. Subway and metro stations are always well-marked. Just follow the signs to your new line and platform.

Bus stops are also marked on Google Maps, and if you're using Google Maps for navigation, it will give you walking directions for the portion of your route between stops. You can also obtain a paper map from the tourist info office and do your navigating the old-school way by looking at cross-streets to determine your location on the map and figuring out which direction you should head to find the next stop.

Almost all of the major cities we have been in allow you 75-90 min to use your ticket on any combination of public transport. If the transport has a validation machine, pop your ticket into it on each leg. My motto: When in doubt, validate.

Hop-On Hop-Off

I know what you are thinking. Those double-decker Hop-On Hop-Off tourist buses can cost around $20 a pop, $40 for two. That's a big chunk of the daily budget just to be carted from tourist attraction to tourist attraction. You know what? You're right, and that's exactly why we don't take them.

Instead, for around the price of three bus/metro tickets, you can buy an all-day pass that allows you to take any mode of public transportation for 24hrs (the buses marked "hop-on hop-off" are not public transportation)! It's a great deal when you are in an enormous city and the sights you want to see are far apart. You may even discover things you wouldn't see on the tourist bus.

"Speaking of unexpected but very cool, you can see many archaeological exhibits for free in Athens. When the subway tunnels were built, shovelful after shovelful of dirt revealed bits of history. Quite a few of the subway stations have displays of the ruins or artifacts found during construction. They are museum-quality exhibits and free to the public. Our favorite stations were Acropoli (the stop for the Acropolis), Syntagma (the stop for the National Garden and Mr. Vertigo), and Monastiraki."

Exploring Athens by Metro

Safety

It must be said that using public transportation comes with inherent risks. Pickpockets are common, and some cities are worse than others. Never let your guard down. Keep your wallet and phone in your front pockets. Don't let your bags out of your sight. Passports and cash exceeding what you plan to use during the day should go into your money belt. If you look like a tourist, you're a target. If you look like a jet-lagged, drunk, or hungover tourist, you're an even bigger target.

In Barcelona, a man on the metro bumped into Pat who in turn bumped into a woman. While the man apologized to Pat for bumping him, the woman put her hand into Pat's pocket. Fortunately, his wallet was in his front pocket and on a leash. Even if she had extricated the wallet, the leash would have alerted him that it was being stolen. (See the Gear chapter: Other Handy Items, for leash info.)

Similarly, a guy on a relatively empty bus in Kuala Lumpur bumped into both of us. My first thought was that he was extremely rude, but a couple of seconds later my jet-lagged brain realized that he had made off with my cell phone. It was already too late, but we jumped off the bus to follow him, but he instantly disappeared into the crowd like a golf ball into the weeds.

These stories aren't meant to dissuade you from using public transportation but are just reminders to take precautions when you do. Being pickpocketed can happen to anyone. Even the venerable Rick Steves fell victim to a pickpocket. Constant vigilance!

Uber / Lyft

Being the tightwads that we are, you probably think we never take a taxi or private car. That isn't true. Sometimes a taxi just makes sense. For example, when we arrive in a city in the middle of the night and have our bags with us, and it's raining, and the Airbnb is 5km away, and the metro has stopped service for the night, then we happily tumble into a big yellow taxi, or any other kind, for that matter.

Sometimes taxis aren't overly expensive, and the comfort-to-expense ratio is high. We are not twenty- or thirty-somethings anymore, or forty-somethings in my case, or fifty-somethings in Pat's case. Let's be honest. Cars are comfortable!

The sharing economy has made ridesharing services like Uber and Lyft a great resource for local transportation and the two companies are similar. First, you download an app to your phone, and then you create an account. After that, you hook your account to a payment method like a credit card, or PayPal, then find a ride.

The apps are easy to use, and you see how much the ride is going to cost up front. Your pick-up location is automatically set to your current location but can be changed in both apps. Also, both Lyft and Uber's apps let you select a four-seat car, a six-seat car, or a high-end car, if they are available. Each app lets you schedule a pick-up time in the future too.

The only drawback is that you really need to have a smartphone with a data plan. I have read that you can use Uber from a computer, but it sounds like more of a hassle than it's worth. In the Technology section of this book, I detail how to buy a SIM card for your out-of-country phone.

Garden-Variety Taxis

We have a serious love-hate relationship with taxis.

> *"Knowing that Brasov is a relatively large city, we expected a sizable train station with an army of taxis stationed just outside prepared for a full-frontal assault*

on anyone resembling a tourist. And that is exactly what we encountered. However, we also received the old price-gouging good cab driver/bad cab driver routine.

Here's how it went down: Our Airbnb host told us to expect to pay between 12 and 15 Leu ($3 to $4 US) for the ride to our Airbnb. When we approached the front-of-the-line taxi driver, he quoted us 50 Leu (~$13 US) and told us that that was the going rate to get into the city center. I started ranting and waving my arms, telling him I would rather walk than get ripped off by him. He smiled and shrugged. Steaming, we walked off and found a shady spot to figure out a plan. Soon, we were approached by another driver who told us that he'd take us into town for 20 Leu. Tired and not willing to squabble over the equivalent of $1.30 US, we agreed and jumped into his cab. A few minutes later, we were at the edge of old town, very near our lodging. I think he felt a tinge of remorse for scamming us because he offered us a big chunk of homemade Romanian bread that he had in the back of the taxi."

Dealing with Taxi Drivers in Romania

Always, always, always agree on a fare before you step into a taxi, or make sure the driver will use the meter. Always! It's also a good idea to ask your host how much you should expect to pay. In the example above, we would have had no idea that the first guy was way off the mark if we didn't have a ballpark number from our host ahead of time.

The best way to avoid getting ripped off is to know what the ride should cost, to agree on that rate before getting into the taxi, to make sure the meter is used if the car is equipped with one, or to have your host arrange a taxi with a company that he or she trusts.

On the "love" end of the love-hate spectrum, we love taxis in countries where the dollar is strong. These old bones can still haul bags onto and off buses and trains and carry them a kilometer or two to our room, but door-to-door service is a luxury that can be affordable in certain parts of the world. Every time the price is right, we opt for a taxi.

Collectivos and Such
In Latin America, in particular, we ran into all means of people-moving. In poorer countries, where owning a car is not so common and the public transportation system is overburdened, private individuals pick up the slack. In Guatemala, pickup trucks with steel cages in the beds run back and forth between nearby towns. You wave one down, jump in the back and hold on to the bars. When you want to be let off, pound on the roof of the cab, then pay the driver.

Collectivos function in the same manner. They stop to pick up anyone who waves them down until they are full, sometimes bursting-at-the-seams full, but they are usually actual cars or minivans. People who operate these types of vehicles have never tried to rip us off. It has either not occurred to them, or we've been lucky, or it's part of their honor-code not to gouge the tourists.

The best way to know where to find the collectivos and how much they cost is to ask a local.

Rickshaws, Pedi-cabs, Tuk-tuks, etc.
If you need a short ride, a rickshaw, pedi-cab, or tuk-tuk may fit the bill. A pedi-cab is a bicycle-powered rickshaw, and a tuk-tuk is basically a scooter-powered rickshaw. They can be lifesavers if you need to haul back a heavy load of groceries in tropical heat, and they can be fun too. Sometimes the driver is chatty and tells you a little about the area or gives some good recommendations for places to see or food to try.

Tuk-tuk drivers can also be a bit annoying. In some countries, it seems that a huge number of people invested in tuk-tuks. They wait outside hotels and hostels in groups and are relentless in their pitches for tours. If you do decide to use a tuk-tuk, just like with a taxi, be sure to agree on a price before getting into one. Avoid accepting a "free" tour. The driver will drag you from tourist trap to tourist trap hoping that you will buy something so that he can make a commission.

Renting a Car

Renting a car gives you so much freedom to explore. Instead of being confined to cities, you can check out small towns and villages or go venture to the middle of nowhere. Sometimes the drive itself is the attraction, like the North Coast 500 in Scotland. Renting a car sounds like a splurge, but it's not unusual to find cars for $12-$20 per day in Europe.

> *"I [Pat] never really thought about or wanted to drive in a country that chose to drive on the left side of the road. It always seemed unnatural to me. But drive I did, totaling over 1500 miles in England and Wales. And to top it off, I did it in a rented Ford Fiesta which had been maintained about as well as a porta-potty at Woodstock. But it was now time to say goodbye to our British Porsche, because we were heading off to Scotland's high country where a real car is a necessity."*

Pat Getting Psyched up for the North Coast 500 in Scotland

A quick note: If you are renting outside of the United States, it is best to know how to drive a manual transmission. The rental car companies usually have automatics, but they are more expensive and in less supply. If you have never driven stick, or failed miserably the first go-around, practice on a friend's car, a really good friend's car, preferably in a deserted parking lot, before you go.

To find the best rates, check at least three different search engines. Some of the better rental car search sites are the following:

- Kayak
- CarRentals.com
- Skyscanner
- Holiday Autos

Picking up and dropping off the car in a major transportation hub will yield lower rates than in a smaller city. Be careful, though, because dropping off the car in a different location than where you picked it up can be exorbitant. Make sure you know what the drop-off charge is. I once priced a one-way car from Spain to Portugal, and all looked good until the very end. The drop-off fee was $600!

Something to keep in mind, too, is that often the rental car companies offer free cancellation up to the day before your reservation. So, if you think you might want to rent a car, reserve early, but don't forget to cancel if you find you won't need the car. You never know, a public transportation strike might happen and then all of a sudden everyone wants to rent a car and there are none to be had.

What about car insurance? Check with your regular car insurance provider to see what, if any, international coverage you have. Also, many credit card companies offer rental car insurance for rentals of up to 30 days. (If you need more than 30 days, have the rental car company bill you in 30-day increments.) Additionally, the insurance that the rental car companies offer is expensive, so if you plan to rent a car, be sure that your regular car insurance covers you or else apply for a credit card that offers rental car insurance (our Chase Marriott card does, even in Ireland). The rental car company may also put a hold on your credit card for the value of the car if you decline their insurance, even if you have coverage through your regular insurance or credit card. This should all be covered in the Terms of Service and be available online.

Speaking of the Terms of Service. Read the fine print! The rental car companies can sneak all kinds of charges in there. If you are under 25 or over 70, a surcharge may apply. On top of that, if the car is returned with a partially full tank, they can charge you for a full tank and apply a service fee. The Terms of Service agreement might also specify that the car is not allowed out of the country. For example, the car we rented in France could not be taken into Spain. It's not as if France and Spain have a discernible border crossing, but if you violate the Terms of Service and have an accident, you are likely to void your insurance. Cars in Italy, for instance, are required to carry snow chains in certain areas during particular months, and some rental companies charge up to $15/day to rent those chains. That's as much as the car itself. Read the fine print! It stinks to be surprised at the rental car desk.

When you approach the rental desk, have these things at hand: your driver's license, your passport, your reservation, a copy of your regular car insurance (if it provides any coverage for international rental cars), and a copy of your credit card insurance coverage provisions. E-copies of these items, other than your ID, are fine, but just be sure to keep your phone charged.

"Pat and the woman reached the part in the contract where they ask if you would like to take their insurance or decline it. Pat declined as usual since our credit card has rental car insurance. That's when things went off the rails. 'You can't decline unless you pay a special processing fee and we put a $5,000 hold on your credit card,' she said in a very rehearsed manner. 'What?' asked Pat agitated. 'My credit card covers rental car insurance,' he said. She went on to explain that practically no credit cards cover rental car insurance in Ireland. Apparently, tourists wreck a lot of cars on the Emerald Isle. Our options were to (a) buy their insurance at $45/day (ha!) (b) pay the decline fee ($35) and have a $5,000 hold on the credit card or (c) get on the phone and confirm that our credit card did in fact cover insurance in Ireland. Well, at least all of the people standing around talking on their cell phones made sense now.

We moved away from the counter to join the cluster of people on their phones. Some of the would-be-car-renters had blank expressions on their faces, some were seemingly on perpetual hold, and others were apparently not getting the news they wanted to hear. What a racket. The rental car companies advertise super-low rates but fail to mention the nearly mandatory, over-priced insurance. We at least had the option of putting a hold on the credit card, but what about people who didn't? Your $14/day car all of a sudden balloons to an almost $60/day one! Ah, good news. After about 15 minutes of navigating the credit card company's options menu, holding, and finally speaking with a representative, we *determined that our credit card did in fact cover Ireland, news that we relayed to the woman handling our contract. She said she still had to charge us the 'processing fee' to decline the insurance. Dirty bat rastards."*

Appreciating the Rental Car Insurance Provided by Our Credit Card - Dublin, Ireland

Finally, when you eventually behold your "new" car, do a thorough inspection for prior damage. Usually, there will be a sheet that you can mark and return to the agent, but, if not, take photos and email them to yourself so that you have a record of the condition the car was in when you received it. You don't want a $500 charge for a crunched bumper that wasn't your doing.

When to Travel

And you thought we were done beating this subject to a pulp, but when to travel is almost as important as how to travel.

Are you renting a car in a large city that you don't know? Pick up and drop off the rental on a weekend, or midday on a weekday, but try to avoid rush hour at all costs. You'll get in the wrong lane at the wrong time, or drive too slowly, or slam on the brakes so you don't miss your turn. You'll be frustrated and won't be endearing yourself to the locals. Worse yet, you may cause an accident. That's no way to start or end a visit.

If you plan to use public transportation on arriving, be sure it is operating at the hour you get there. Buses, trains, and metros rarely run 24/7, and service to suburban towns and villages can become spotty, even as early as dinner-time. Weekends and holidays often have reduced service, but you may encounter fewer people than on a workday. Of course, if it is a popular holiday, you may experience many more travelers. Again, avoid rush hour. It is really no fun to lug your bags onto a crowded metro and through a station teeming with people.

"In the morning we said our goodbyes and rode down to the bus stop with Francesco. The bus was there, but not the driver. Francesco asked a man sitting at the bus stop what the situation was. Based on Francesco's expression, the response was obviously nothing good. Wonderful. Now what had Rossibus done? The man told Francesco that the bus wasn't running that day. Francesco pressed him for more information, but I don't think two words were given. Francesco returned to the car and said, 'No problem! I will drive you to the train station.' What luck. We had nearly declined the ride to the bus stop because it was so near. We'd probably still be sitting at the bus stop if Francesco hadn't been there.

Small towns are great, and we loved Sacrofano, but they can present some challenges too. Relying on public transportation in the outskirts requires patience and the kindness of strangers. Luckily we had both."

The Pitfalls of Using Public Transport in the Suburbs - Sacrofano, Italy

In a broader context, you can save a lot of money and avoid the crowds if you travel in the shoulder-season or off-season. Keep in mind, the weather may not be as wonderful, and some towns may even become virtual ghost-towns in the off-season.

Accommodations

"We arrived at our Airbnb in Moyard and were welcomed with a fire in the peat-burning stove, a loaf of homemade bread, and preserves. It was wet and cold so the fire was very much appreciated and the bread smelled wonderful. There was no sense trying to get a hike in since it was raining cats and dogs, so off to the pub we went.

Our host gave us the run-down on the nearby pubs. We opted for Molly's which she had described as a quirky locals' place. She was right. The locals were a bit quirky, but thoroughly entertaining. They occupied every stool at the bar, so we took a seat at a table, sipped on our Guinnesses (Guinneess? Guinnii?), and watched and listened."

Feeling at Home in Moyard, Ireland

Finding a place to stay on a modest budget can be a bit of a challenge, but options for an inexpensive roof over your head almost always exist. As mentioned before, our budget is $100/day for the two of us. That includes food, transportation, sightseeing, booze, and lodging. On average, we try to keep our lodging at 20-25% of our budget, and the key words once again are "on average."

One of the best ways to find economical lodging, as well as everything else, as I've remarked before, is to travel to countries where the dollar is strong. Southeast Asia, Southeast Europe, and Central America are all good candidates right now. For example, in Vietnam nearly every room we took was priced in the mid-teens in dollars, and most included a hot breakfast. Though basic, they were clean rooms with a private bath and hot water. One room with an amazing view of a karst-filled bay on Cát Bà Island was only $6/night. If you are not sure how strong the dollar is where you want to go, pull up Booking.com or one of the other lodging search engines (Expedia, Priceline, Kayak, etc.) and see what a room goes for in dollars or your native currency.

Types of Accommodations

Accommodations for every budget are available almost anywhere you go.

Hotels

The first thing that leaps to mind for accommodation is a hotel. They are often palaces of luxury with legions of lounge chairs surrounding pools, lavender-scented spas, state-of-the-art gyms, gourmet restaurants with stunning views, and a swim-up bar. The rooms have Wi-Fi, A/C, heat, 8,000 cable tv stations on a tv as large as the wall, a beautiful jetted bathtub, and super-comfy beds with a "pillow bar." Though hotels may be the first things that leap to mind, they are rarely where we stay due to their budget-breaking price tag.

From time to time, we do splurge and stay in a hotel, but we have a little secret. The secret is that we use the Chase Marriott credit card for as many purchases as possible. After saving up enough points for three nights, we book four, using points for three and cash for one. In effect, the room costs ¼ its regular rate per night. That still might mean $40-$50 per night, but we keep other expenses low. It's wonderful to be pampered from time to time because life as a vagabond can have its discomforts. After a few weeks in nostels, lots of walking, hiking, camping, and multi-day bus rides, it's time for pristine sheets, ice cubes, and a jacuzzi.

> *"The bellhops were always curious when we checked into a Marriott with backpacks on our backs, overgrown hair, and the look of having spent the past few nights sleeping in our clothes. We probably didn't smell great either. One of them always summoned the courage to ask us what the deal was, and we would tell them about our lifestyle and latest travels. We often spent half an hour or so chatting with them."*

At the Santiago Marriott

Timeshares

No! Do not buy a timeshare week! But they are a good option to rent in some cases. If you can find a studio or one-bedroom unit, you can do pretty well, and if you are traveling with another couple, or two, and can split the cost, they can really make a lot of sense. Timeshare owners are stuck if they can't use their week because they still have to pay their annual maintenance fee. That fee can be around $600 or $700 per week. Often you can find timeshare units listed on Craigslist in the States for the amount of the maintenance fee. The owners just want to hang onto the unit and pass on the fee and week to you. Timeshares still count as a splurge in our books, but if you have the means, they are a good choice. Usually they will include quite a few amenities such as pools, grills, a game room, a gym, recreational activities, that sort of stuff.

Apartments

A great way to receive good rates and to experience the true flavor of an area is to stay in one place for a full week or, better yet, a full month. Frequently, especially with Airbnb, weekly and monthly discounts apply. Think France is expensive? Back in 2016 we were able to find a one-bedroom apartment on Airbnb with a full kitchen in Perpignan. It was within walking distance of anything we needed: butcher, veggie market, historic downtown, bakery, hypermarché, etc. The damage? $700/month. That's a little over $23/day. Not bad. A ton of money was saved and we had a lot of fun going to the markets and cooking for ourselves. As an added bonus, we made lifelong friends with the owner, who lived in the flat above.

Hostels
Don't automatically dismiss hostels. Sure, I know, we all love having a private bathroom. The thought of sharing a bathroom with who knows how many people isn't overly appealing, and sleeping in a room full of scratching, snoring college boys is even less so. The fact is, many hostels also have double rooms with private baths. Sometimes, though, even they are too far above our budget. On a couple of occasions, we even opted to sleep in the dorm room. When we were visiting El Calafate and Ushuaia, Argentina, in the dead of summer (January) and the peak of tourist season, a dorm bed was around $15/person, so you can imagine what a double-room with private bath was going for!

So, what was the dorm room experience like? It really wasn't bad, and hostels in general have quite a few perks. In the first case, we were in a two-bunk room, and in the second we were in a four-bunk room. For the most part, our dorm-mates were respectful of each other's space and were polite. The only issue we had was in the two-bunk room when a couple of women from Spain moved in and figured it was fine to talk on their cell phones in the middle of the night to friends and relatives waking up back home.

As for the perks, the hostels had shared kitchens and a communal area. Having access to a kitchen meant we were able to go to the market and cook our own food rather than eat at the outrageously expensive restaurants. People of all ages from all over the world were doing the same as us. Ok, they were mostly younger, but we weren't out of place. After dinner we would crack out our Farkel game and teach the others how to play. Everyone brought a bottle or two of great Argentine wine to share and a willingness to converse. The topics usually went straight to the taboo ones of politics and religion. Travelers are a curious sort. They like to discuss the subjects most people tend to avoid when chatting with strangers.

One surprising thing to note is that sometimes hostels have an included "medical benefit," unlike the high-priced hotels. Once, when we were in Tarija, Bolivia, we went to a huge party where the nuns of Tarija kicked our butts at beer pong (true story). Much sharing of liquor-filled vessels occurred, and a few germs must have been sipped up in the action. The next day we left for Salta, Argentina, and, through sheer luck or possibly divine intervention, decided to stay at a hostel other than the one where we had reserved. A woman in the Salta bus station greeted us on our arrival, touted her hostel, and offered a room with a private bath at the same rate as the shared bathroom room at the hostel we had originally chosen. When she showed us her binder of photos and amenities, we both noticed something about medical coverage but didn't give it much thought. Private bath? Of course we took it!

Within a couple of days, I had developed a serious case of bronchitis and laryngitis and plummeted into a fever and phlegm-filled abyss, likely from too much sharing of liquor-filled vessels back in Bolivia. Pat thought I was going to die, so he asked the owners about seeing a doctor, or undertaker, or something. I didn't actually hear him since I was busy trying not to die. Instead of us going to a doctor's office, the doctor came to the hostel. He examined me, gave me a shot in the butt with antibiotics and left. No charge. It was part of our budget-friendly hostel room rate. Awesome!

Camping
I'm not pretending to be an expert on camping, but it is an option and in some cases it is the only way to see a place. Since camping gear is bulky and heavy, we don't carry it with us, but we have rented gear from outfitters. In Chile we rented a tent, stove, sleeping bags, etc. to do the "W" in Torres del Paine National Park. The "W" is a four-day trek through mountains, across rivers, and over glaciers, culminating in views of the massive stone towers, or torres, for which the park was named. Camping is the best way to experience the park on a budget. At one point in the trek, we each feared that the other had fallen off a cliff and drowned in the lake below. That's not really a selling point, but we both survived, and it was a spellbinding park.

170

"Well, we made it to the first camp in about five hours, all 18 kilometers! But not without some excitement right at the end. Carrie was still trailing me by a good distance for fear that all the crankiness hadn't dissipated. The last 300 yards of the hike had a trail along a cliff above the lake which quickly descended to the camping area. The wind, howling, was trying to blow us off the trail into the lake a few hundred feet below. I didn't care. I could see the camp. I was on a mission. Just get me there! Please, just get me there. Feats (feets?) don't fail me now.

About half way down I decided to wait for Carrie, knowing that she had a fear of heights. After about 10 minutes, NO Carrie! Was she lost, eaten by wolves? I panicked, threw off my pack and sprinted back up the trail, all the time yelling, 'Carrie! Carrie!' Nothing. I ran into a fellow hiker. Chinese! In my best Chinese, I asked if he'd seen a gringo woman. 'No,' he replied, so I bolted towards camp to get help. I looked down at the camp and saw Carrie scampering my way, yelling: 'Pat! Pat!' Long story short, she had found an easier safer way to get to camp and by now thought I was dead and in the lake. Now we were both cranky, but all was well. We had made it. Soon we had the tent set up, had a scotch in hand, and had a spectacular view! Ahhh... who can stay cranky? Life is good!"

Backpacking in Torres del Paine

When you plan to take some time to go camping, it's a good idea to book a room at the same place on both ends of your camping trip. You don't want to drag all of your clothing and stuff with you, especially if you are backpacking. Whenever we have asked to leave bags until we return, the request has always been granted, and nothing has ever been stolen (knock on wood). Please don't leave anything valuable behind, though!

Guesthouses, Homestays, Motels, Inns, etc.

Wherever you go, a category of lodging intended for the budget-minded traveler exists. Usually, they are small and family-run. In India, they are often called "homestays," in many parts of the world, they are called "guesthouses." In the States and Europe, you have "motels" and "inns." If for some reason you arrive somewhere without a reservation, look for those terms if you want an inexpensive room. Be sure to inspect the room before you take it if you don't have the benefit of reading reviews ahead of time.

Private Rooms
Airbnb has revolutionized budget traveling. Not only can you rent a whole house or an apartment, but you can rent a guest room in someone's house. This option was invaluable in the UK and Ireland where the dollar wasn't strong (pre-Brexit especially) and basic motels were $75-$100. No two of our experiences were alike, but I can only think of one bad experience and many great ones.

In Bath, England, we were welcomed by a friendly couple to their newly renovated home, a beautifully converted stable. The guest room was spacious and comfortable, and a bathroom was dedicated for guest use only. Their cat was as sweet and as friendly as they come. We also hit it off with the couple and spent the night pub-hopping with them. (The cat stayed home.) In the mornings, fruit, yogurt, crumpets, English muffins, fresh juice, and eggs were set out for breakfast.

In Galway, Ireland, we had a small but comfortable room and shared the only bathroom with a young Scottish couple and their baby. The five of us ate breakfast together each day, cereal and coffee for the adults, you-know-what for the baby. They were interesting and well-educated, and we enjoyed pleasant conversation with them. We chatted each morning until it was time for him to go to work, her to school, and the baby to grandma's, and then we went off and explored Galway.

In Liverpool, England, we had a large room in an attic and a bathroom to ourselves. The owners weren't around much, but the room had a "breakfast bar." It consisted of the smallest refrigerator I have ever seen in my life. It was large enough to hold a pint of milk, and that's exactly what it held.

A basket contained boxes of cereal, packets of pastries, tea, and instant coffee.

Each stay had its own character, its own vibe. The interactions with the owners were always different and usually interesting. Sometimes breakfast was included and sometimes not. Some rooms had a private bathroom while others had a shared bathroom. One thing all of our successful private room stays had in common was plenty of positive reviews.

I don't know what travel rule it is, but it's certainly near the top: Be sure to read the reviews, and avoid places with few or no reviews! As mentioned at the beginning of this section, we had only good experiences, except for one, and that was completely avoidable. In Cambridge, we needed a place that was in our budget and close enough to town so we could walk. Only a few options came up in the search. In the end, we picked a room with only one review, and that review was poorly written at that. The room and house were a disaster. Lesson learned. Never select a room, or apartment, or hotel for that matter, without reading a sufficient number of reviews!

> *"After our host left, we took a more thorough look at the place. The bathroom was filthy. There were hairs and grime from at least a thousand other guests caked on the floor and in the tub. Other people's toiletries were scattered everywhere. There was no toilet paper. The light in our bedroom didn't work. The kitchen was gross. A once-white electric kettle stood on the dingy counter like a mangy old dog. Nope. This wasn't going to work.*
>
> *I messaged the host through Airbnb to tell her we were bailing. I described the scene with CSI-like objectivity. She said she'd send her husband over later with toilet paper and a lightbulb. She clearly had missed my point. She claimed that 'the other guests made the house dirty' and, 'it wasn't her responsibility.' What? No way were we staying in that petri dish of who knows what. We left*

promptly and checked into a Travelodge we had noticed
earlier from the pub. Hopefully we hadn't already
contracted a super-virus or something."

**Learning That Listings with Few Reviews Should
Be Avoided Like a 10-Story Walk-up**

Other People's Homes (Pet sitting)

When we arrived in the UK, we were a little bit shocked that half or more of our budget would be going toward our room each day. That didn't leave a lot of pub or fun money, so we had to figure out something else. Camping? Not in the UK, not for me. I swear it rained every day and it was never north of chilly. Couchsurfing? No, we still haven't tried crashing on someone's couch. Sounds like it's more for the gap-year kids with a $10 budget. That is when we discovered TrustedHouseSitters.com.

TrustedHouseSitters matches pet sitters with people who need someone to watch their pets and home while they go off on vacation. It's really a great service for both parties. For the owner, the pets stay in their own home instead of going to a kennel. If the pet needs medication or has special requirements, or if plants need to be watered, the pet sitter takes care of it. In return, the pet sitter gets free lodging and a temporary furry friend. It's brilliant!

Besides that, it's easy to sign up for. The first step is to have a few people write referrals for you. If you've pet sat before, ask those people to write one for you. If you haven't pet sat, ask for character references that say how reliable and neat you are. If you have your own pets, have a friend write a referral saying how loving and caring you are and how happy your pet is.

Next, join one of the pet sitting services. We joined TrustedHouseSitters, because it is the largest and has a good reputation. Joining TrustedHouseSitters will set you back about $120 for a year-long membership, but if the going rate for lodging is $60/night, you only have to pet sit for two nights to break even. In 2016, we pet sat for a total of six weeks and that significantly lowered our average room rate.

Tools for Finding Accommodations

I use a limited bag of tricks for finding accommodations, but they complement each other well.

Booking.com

My go-to app is Booking.com. The app makes searching for an accommodation easy. To use it, just plug in the city/town where you intend to stay, the check-in and check-out dates, the number of people, and then click the "Let's Go!" button. A list of properties will be displayed that you can sort by ratings, distance to the center of town, lowest price first (my favorite), and more. You are also able to filter the results to include preferred amenities such as free parking and Wi-Fi, and to select a price range. Speaking of price, don't freak out when you see what appears to be a high nightly rate. If your stay is more than one night, the rate shown is for the entire stay.

The default view of the search results is a list of the properties, but you can use the map view to see where the rooms are located. Click on the little blue dots on the map and you'll get a quick-view of the property you've selected, which includes the property's rating and cost for the stay. When you find a property you like, click on either the quick-view or the name in the list to see photos, reviews, and the types of rooms available. To make a reservation, click "Reserve," and follow the instructions to complete your reservation. A confirmation will be sent to your email, and your booking will also be stored on your phone, so you'll always have the information (address, phone number, email, etc.) that you need to find your room.

After your stay, you will be asked to write a review. Please complete the review and be honest. Travelers, yourself included, rely upon accurate reviews. Speaking of your stay, with Booking.com after five stays you earn what they call "genius status." With genius status, some properties offer discounts, free cancellation, a free breakfast, or other incentives to entice genius members to book with them. That's why it's a good idea to pick one booking service and stick with it.

Airbnb.com

I honestly can't say enough good things about Airbnb. The whole "sharing economy" has made traveling much more affordable and even more interesting. Meeting wonderful people, staying in amazing homes, and living like the locals are some of the things that make Airbnb special.

The Airbnb app is, in many ways, similar to the booking.com app. You plug in the city/town, the check-in and check-out dates, the number of people, and you can set filters and indicate a price range if you like. The properties come up in a list, but unlike Booking.com, you can't sort the list by price or by ratings. When you switch to map-view, the approximate location of the property is marked with a box containing the price. That's convenient, but notice that I said "approximate location." Airbnb does not give you the exact address until you make the reservation.

When you find the property that you are interested in booking, click "Request to Book." Airbnb is a little bit different in that the owner of the property has the option to accept your request or deny it. Well, why would they deny your request? You see, after you stay at an Airbnb property not only are you asked to review the property, but your host is asked to review you. If you have a long list of reviews indicating that you are messy, noisy, or disrespectful, you can count on being denied a reservation.

Another unique characteristic of Airbnb is that the owner of the property has 24 hours to accept or reject your request. Why would they wait? Well, if you are booking only one or two nights, the owner may want to see if a longer reservation comes in. I can't blame an owner for doing that. Turning a room over is work. Nevertheless, the 24-hour waiting period can present some problems if you're making a reservation that starts in the next few days, but there are a couple of ways to deal with it. The most straightforward way is to turn on the "Instant Book" filter. With "Instant Book" turned on, the search will return only properties where the owner has waived the 24-hour period, and your request will be automatically accepted.

An alternate way around the 24-hour waiting period is to ask the host a question through an Airbnb message (there is a link right on the page with the property description). When you ask a question, the host is obliged to respond quickly and might read the reviews that other hosts have written about you. If your reviews are good, the host can opt to give you 24 hours to make a reservation. Now the shoe is on the other foot. This gives you the right, for 24 hours, but not the obligation, to rent the property. It's like buying a call option on a stock. This little trick is also handy when you find a property you really like and another one that would do. Ask a question of both hosts, and maybe they will both give you 24 hours to decide.

Once you have your reservation, the Airbnb app makes it easy to contact your host through the built-in messenger feature. This is the preferred method of communication since, if any problems arise, there will be a record of the messages. The messaging feature has a unique notification sound to let you know when a message, or a confirmation, or other communication, has arrived. On a related note, only book an Airbnb accommodation through Airbnb. Do not make a side-deal directly with the host. The reason is that although you may think you are getting a great deal, all of the protection in the form of insurance provided by Airbnb will be non-existent.

Another difference from Booking.com is that Airbnb offers "Experiences." An Experience may be a photo-walk, a guided hike, or a gastro-tour, each of which is offered by a local. On the Airbnb home screen, click "Experiences" and then enter the city, date, and number of guests. In Diacceto, Italy, our host had plans of offering a tour of a small, non-touristy, part of Tuscany through Airbnb Experiences. We were fortunate in that he asked us to be his guinea pigs so that he could test-drive his tour. It was a wonderful day of sightseeing and eating and drinking local specialties!

Kayak.com
Kayak is another good resource for rooms, flights, and rental cars. It combs through multiple search engines (Booking.com, Hotels.com, Priceline, etc.) so that you can

see all of the inventory and rates. Kayak sometimes finds lower room rates than Booking.com, but more often than not the rates aren't terribly different, or the best deal is Booking.com anyway. Since we are Booking.com genius members, I check Kayak only when I can't find anything I like with Booking.com or Airbnb.

Google Maps

It has happened on a few occasions that Booking.com and Airbnb do not have a lot of listings in our price range. When that happens, which is rare, Google Maps is the next choice (web and mobile app are both excellent). Pull up the city or town you plan to stay in, and then search "hotels" and keep zooming in. Most of the time the room rate will be displayed as well as a description of the property, in addition to some reviews. A link to the hotel's website or to the booking service they use will also be provided. If you don't find it with a Booking.com search, it may be because the property is only listed with Priceline, Expedia, Hotels, or some other service. Some hotels don't use a booking service at all, so you either need to call them directly or contact them through their website. Google Maps was invaluable for finding accommodations while driving Scotland's North Coast 500 in the summer. Rooms were scarce, and the ones on Booking.com evaporated like a single malt scotch set in front of me.

TrustedHouseSitters.com

At the time of writing, TrustedHouseSitters provides only a webpage, but it scales pretty well onto a mobile device's browser, and it's easy to use. The developers are continuously upgrading the user experience, making it easier to find the pet sit you want. The service is extremely popular in the UK and US, with a few hundred pet sits listed at any given time.

You can select the type of animal you'd like to sit and when and where you'd like to do the sitting, but the key is to be flexible. When we were looking for pet sits, we were flexible on location and length of stay because cat sits are less available than dog sits. Let's face it, cats are much easier and, unless they have special requirements, cats can be left alone for much of the day.

A word of caution, though, applying for a pet sit and actually being selected can take some time. When we were planning to go to the UK, we applied to many pet sits before we lined up our first one, so we kept applying until we had three lined up for a total of six weeks. 'Last minute' pet sits also came up on TrustedHousesitters, so we kept an eye on those too. The pet sits became our destinations, and we filled in the time between with Airbnbs or whatever we found on Booking.com.

> *"The home was bright with lots of windows that took full advantage of the outdoor beauty. There were multiple areas inside and outside to sit, relax, and take it all in. Charlie would let us know when we were 'doing it wrong.' Apparently, mornings were supposed to be spent in the upstairs living room and not the downstairs dining room. At least we agreed that happy hour should be spent outside in the garden."*

Pet Sitting Charlie, an 18-year-old Burmese, in Pembrokeshire, Wales

Cheap Eats and Discount Drinks

"The tourist map was awesome. Let's see, a street labeled 'Night Food' and one marked 'Morning Food.' Nice! We arrived at the market in the early evening while things were still getting set up. Nearby, we found a restaurant with a good vantage point for observing the activity at the market. The vendors fired up their grills and brought huge pots of who-knows-what to a simmer while the tourists and locals milled about, and we sipped on cold BeerLaos. After a short while, the people-watching and tantalizing smells made us hungry, so we finished our beers and then wandered down 'Night Food' Street.

Stalls packed what appeared more of an alley than a street. There were countless food options: meat-on-a-stick, fresh green papaya salad, dumplings, noodle soups, and more. We pushed through the crowd from one end to the other to see what there was to eat. When we ran out of stalls, we turned around and started ordering one of this and one of that until we had a bag full of goodies for dinner.

At the end of the food stalls were women frying up fluffy, little, coconutty, custard-filled cakes about the size of an obese quarter. Obviously, we made room in our bag. It turned out that they were one of Pat's favorite treats."

Finding Cheap and Delicious Food in Luang Prabang, Laos

Much of the intrigue of traveling is in tasting new foods and sampling new drinks. Being budget-travelers, though, you can't exactly eat in a Michelin-starred restaurant every evening, and ordering a brilliantly presented four-course, culinary delight accompanied by a bottle of wine rated 99 in the Wine Spectator is probably only a once-a-year possibility. Cooking for yourself is a budget-friendly option, but preparing the same dishes you know how to fix at home, albeit with local produce and maybe a few creative substitutions, isn't the same as experiencing the local cuisine.

Countries where the dollar is strong are ideal for sampling a range of local foods and beverages. In fact, in much of Southeast Asia, Latin America, and parts of Europe, it doesn't pay to cook for yourself, but if you find yourself in a country where going to a restaurant is a budget-bender, there are ways to taste the local fare and keep the costs down.

Street Food

Don't fear the street cart or makeshift grill! These are where the locals go to pick up affordable "fast food." You never know what you might find, but look for the longest line and get in it. High volume means fresh food. The locals know the best taste and value, so follow their lead. In Puerto Montt, Chile, we came across long lines of hungry people waiting in front of meat-on-a-stick covered smoking grills. It smelled fantastic, and it was... and cheap too. The grills were conveniently set up just outside of a grocery store, so it was easy to supplement the mouth-watering strips of protein with some veggies and a bottle of Chilean wine.

In Panama City, a Jamaican named Marcos ran our favorite street cart and offered "Fish in a Bag." We found him by word of mouth from other travelers. The fish was Jamaican-jerk-seasoned, battered and deep-fried, and then served with patacones (sliced, smashed, and deep-fried green plantains). Marcos' homemade and delightfully tongue-torturing habanero sauce was sparingly applied, and the meal was served in, you guessed it, a paper bag.

Florence, Italy, had carts selling lampredotto, a hot and juicy sandwich made from the stewed fourth stomach of a cow. I hear you. It sounds gross, but it was divine and insanely popular with the locals. I had read about the sandwich in a guidebook, then searched for the best in Florence and eventually found a cart. I could go on and on about the wonderful food we have eaten from carts, but you get the idea. Just make sure there are plenty of locals eating from the cart and you'll have nothing to fear.

Occasionally, the street food finds you. In Mendoza, Argentina, we were sitting in a bar nursing beers and chatting with the bartender when a vendor with a basket of piping-hot empanadas attracted our attention. We watched him make his way past the tables and towards us at the bar. Everyone at the tables bought at least one empanada, so we bought some too. They were delicious! Juicy, steaming beef, onion, egg, olives, and spices that screamed, "You're not in Kansas anymore!" filled the small dough pockets. My only regret is that we bought only two and never had the good fortune of running into the empanada-man again.

Bus stops are another place where you can often find vendors hawking inexpensive hand-held snacks. In Ecuador, sliced green mango with chili powder was one of my favorite snacks. The first time I saw the cart of plastic bags on ice with slices of something green in them, I had no idea what the green slices were. What I did know was that a lot of people were buying bags, sprinkling a red powder on the slices, and eating them with obvious delight. That was enough reason for me to buy a bag. They were a wonderful treat, slightly sour, salty and spicy, and a much healthier snack than a bag of finger-staining orange cheesy-poofs.

You can even find street food right on buses and trains too. Vendors with baskets or coolers often jump on at one stop and then offer their goodies up and down the aisle. They get off a stop or two later and head back in the other direction on the next bus or train, going back and forth until they run out of food. In India, samosas were commonly offered (a sort of an Indian version of an empanada). In Thailand, refreshing ice-cold coconut water right in the coconut was popular. In Mexico, churros kept people with a sweet tooth happy. If it is obvious that you "are not from here," don't be surprised if a local buys something and offers you a taste of it. Try it. You might like it!

Markets

Markets aren't always just stalls of raw foods. Frequently, there are counters or restaurants right inside the market, serving hot, fresh, and affordable food. The people manning the stalls need to eat too, you know, and since the ingredients are at hand, and there is a captive audience, it's apropos to have restaurants in the market.

In Ensenada, Mexico, seafood restaurants surrounded the fish market. Ceviche and fish tacos couldn't get any fresher. In Tarija, Bolivia, the back-end of the market was full of rudimentary restaurants with cauldrons of bubbling saice (sigh-say) sitting on portable propane burners. The saice at our favorite "restaurant," where we'd eat with strangers at communal tables, was an amazingly flavorful dish consisting of ground beef, peas, onions, and an unfamiliar, but addictive, seasoning. Sliced onions and tomatoes fresh from the fields topped the dish. Pat's favorite vendor, though, was on the other side of the market, the flan woman! She'd see him coming and have his cup of flan ready before he even got there.

As mentioned in the blog clip at the beginning of this chapter, in Luang Prabang, Laos, "morning food" and "night food" had designated markets. Our host gave us a map that showed where they were. They were popular with tourists and locals alike, and with good reason. The food was inexpensive, fresh, and there were so many options of new and unfamiliar foods to taste. Mekong river weed? Of course I tried it and I liked it!

Obviously, you can always make a meal out of fresh produce and cold snacks found in markets. Buy some hard salami, cheese, olives, apples, and carrots, and then throw in a baguette or a flatbread. Now you have a decent meal. Sometimes seafood vendors will steam shrimp for you so the shrimp are ready to be peeled and eaten. Or, perhaps the fishmonger might shuck oysters so you can slurp them right there, or he may package them with ice to be taken away.

Upon arriving in a new city, we search out the main market, even if only to walk through it. In Athens, Greece, the market was huge with display after display of meat, seafood, fruit, and vegetables. Restaurants with menus on chalkboards were clustered inside too. We were even treated to unexpected entertainment on the day we went to explore.

> *"Having checked the Acropolis off of our to-do list, it was time for the serious sights - the meat, fish, and veggie markets. We love food almost as much as wine, and the markets did not disappoint. The meat and fish markets were clean and well-lit. The offerings were proudly displayed in refrigerated glass cabinets or on ice. The butchers all seemed to have a sense of humor, hamming it up with their big cleavers raised at passers-by. The fishmongers were less aggressive, but possibly a bit OCD. Some of their displays were amazingly intricate works of art. Of course, cats went where they wished and were well-fed on scraps and offal.*
>
> *Without warning, a two-piece band set up in the meat market and a troupe of people in traditional dress showed up. The aisle between the meat counters was*
>
> *cleared to make space, and a grill full of sausages smoked nearby. The dancers took the 'stage' and danced in the traditional way to the sounds of the two-piece band. We*

were entertained. The cats were sated and pleased. It was an unexpected, but very Athenian, way to spend the afternoon."

Exploring the Market in Athens, Greece

Happy Hour

As you would probably guess, happy hour is my favorite time of day. After a long day of walking around and taking in the sights, it is definitely time for an adult beverage. In Asia, much of Latin America, and in parts of Europe, it is an inexpensive indulgence to pop into a bar or restaurant and order a beer. A glass of wine is usually budget-friendly too, if you are in a country that produces wine, but cocktails can be pricey, especially if the spirit you want isn't what the locals drink. For instance, in Mexico, don't order a scotch. That's made in Scotland, which is a long way away. Instead, stick to tequila-based cocktails. In Nicaragua, go with rum, and in Peru, choose pisco. All of those spirits have varying degrees of quality, and a price to match, so make sure the bartender isn't pouring you a rum and coke with a top-shelf rum at a top-shelf price!

The best part about happy hour isn't only that it's time to have a drink. It's also the time of day when many bars, pubs, tavernas, cantinas, etc. offer discounted prices on drinks and food. Sometimes there are two-for-one drinks, half-priced appetizers, cheap pints, or even a small buffet of finger-foods.

The masters of the happy hour are the Spaniards, however. In many cities in Spain, when you order a drink, a free snack comes with it. I'm not talking about small bowls of Chex Mix either. I'm talking about generous snacks. You've heard of them, I'm sure. They're called "tapas." Tapas can be almost anything, but popular ones include patatas bravas (fried potato wedges with a garlic aioli), albóndigas (meatballs), gambas al ajillo (shrimp in garlic sauce), calamares (fried squid), jamón Iberico (thinly sliced cured ham). The list goes on. Though the tapas aren't free in every Spanish city, they are still an affordable way to make a meal out of multiple small dishes. It's a lot of fun too because you get to taste many traditional treats.

Eat a Big Lunch

Wait. What? I thought we were trying to save money, not buy more food. Well, have you ever read both the lunch and dinner menu at a restaurant? If you have, you inevitably noticed that the prices on the lunch menu are less expensive than on the dinner menus. But aren't the portions smaller at lunchtime? Not necessarily. In fact, sometimes you get more food at lunchtime. As an example, we had a favorite hole-in-the-wall Chinese restaurant (now defunct) in Flagstaff, Arizona, that offered a limited choice of lunch specials. All of the specials came with a pot of tea, soup, salad, fried wontons, and rice. Without fail, by the time my entrée would arrive, I was nearly full. It was a lot of food and enough to take home for a second meal. On the dinner menu, though, the same entrée cost more. To be fair, it may have been a bit larger, but none of the sides, other than rice, came with the meal. Dinner was significantly more expensive and no more filling, especially when you add in that we'd have a cocktail with our meal instead of tea.

So, where do you find the great lunch deals? If you are in a working city or in the working section of a tourist city, look for where the laborers go at lunchtime. Fishermen, construction workers, people who do physical labor all day, need a stick-to-your-ribs meal at lunchtime. Scan the parking lots for work trucks. People who work with their muscles all day seek out restaurants with large portions and small prices. Often, there will be a special of the day, plat du jour (France), almuerzo (Latin America), etc. The meals usually consist of two or three courses with a soft drink/wine/beer, and are the best value. And because they are meant to fill the bellies of people burning a lot of calories, you may have enough for a second meal.

That brings me to another point. When you are traveling, there are times when you won't have a way to save your leftovers. To avoid wasting food (that's one of my pet-peeves... that and the TSA, of course) order an appetizer instead of an entrée. Or, since this book is geared toward couples, share a lunch. If it turns out to be not enough food, you can always order an extra cup of soup, a side-salad, or, of course, a dessert. Now that you have eaten a hearty meal, you can eat lightly at dinnertime, and maybe even be satisfied with eating street food or snacks from the market. Buy your beverage of choice at the grocery store, and you're all set.

Restaurants

Did you honestly think that I could go through a chapter without mentioning Google Maps? Come on, I know you've been paying attention... Anyway, the search "nearby" feature of Google Maps allows you to search for things generically, such as "restaurants." The restaurants will show up on the map, and a list will be provided. In the one-stop-shopping nature of Google Maps, you can see ratings, hours, and most importantly, reviews where you can generally learn if the restaurant is over-priced or budget-friendly.

Food Festivals

Granted, food festivals may not provide the least expensive meal you can have, but they are a great way to taste many dishes that are prepared by people who make a specific dish their specialty. Stop by a tourist office, or ask your host to find out if one will be in town while you are there. In Lima, Peru, the chef of the Yacht Club Peruano invited us to a food festival. We quickly accepted, as we had come to love Peruvian food in our time there, and... Travel Rule #1 compelled it. Peruvian food is without a question some of the best food on the planet, by the way.

Food festivals all work pretty similarly. There are rows of tents with nose-grabbing smells emanating from steaming trays or smoking grills. Toque-topped people serve up samples of the delightful delectables. You either pay directly at the tent for a taste or buy tickets from a central cashier and hand over a ticket. As a couple, you can sample twice as many plates as an individual, if you share. My favorite dish at the Lima food festival was the rocoto relleno, a stuffed red pepper. Ah, but this wasn't your grandma's stuffed pepper. This pepper would knock your granny clean out of her rocking chair. The rocoto looks a lot like a red bell pepper, but it's a pepper with a force to be reckoned with. The beauty of the dish is that the chopped beef, ground nuts, condensed milk, diced olives, boiled egg, raisin-sweetened filling, snuggled under a blanket of melted cheese, balance the sting of the menacing rocoto pepper nicely. As a precaution, though, keep a beer nearby, or, if you are particularly sensitive to spicy foods, make it a glass of milk instead!

Tipping

I guess this is as good a spot as any to discuss tipping. In the States we tip 15-20% at restaurants, but don't assume it's that way everywhere. Ask around, check your guidebook, and be sure to tip what is customary for where you are. There are many countries where 10% is expected, others where only leftover change is, and in others still, tipping is not done at all and is actually considered downright rude. Don't under-tip or over-tip.

Thank You

Dear Reader, thank you for purchasing this book and taking the time to read it to the end. Of course, you may have just fallen asleep on the "turn page" button and arrived here too. Hopefully, you got here in the former manner, though, and picked up some strategies and tips to make your next adventure more comfortable and less expensive.

I hope that you enjoyed the stories from our travels, too, and are excited to get out there and make your own memories.

I encourage you to remember Travel Rule #1:
If a local asks if you want to do something or go somewhere, say yes!

Thank you again, and If you enjoyed this book please consider leaving a review.

If you have questions or comments, send me an email at: carrie.kinnison@gmail.com

53193291R00106

Made in the USA
Middletown, DE
11 July 2019